SECRET
AFFAIRS
OF THE
SOUL

Also by Paul Hawker

SOUL SURVIVOR

A Spiritual Quest Through Forty Days &
Forty Nights of Mountain Solitude

Praise for *Soul Survivor*

With gentle, visual language, Hawker allows us to
vicariously climb the pinnacles and stand on the edge
where 200 kph winds may kick up at any moment.
We are left with a contact high. – NAPRA ReView

Readers will find Hawker's mountain trek a thrilling
affair – and it is precisely that: an affair with the Voice
that convinces him he is loved. [This book] ought to be on
everyone's "must read" list." – Prairie Messenger

Inspiring and down-to-earth...shows by example how he
worked through the mind chatter to listen to the voices
within. – Issues

Soul Survivor *is a suspenseful and intensely gripping read. I*
was awed and enthralled by this film maker's honest quest.
– Journey

The narrative is finely written, fast-flowing and with expert
film-maker's clarity. It is a book which should encourage
readers to seek the time alone with God in silent retreat.
– Anglican Encounter

PAUL HAWKER

SECRET AFFAIRS

OF THE

SOUL

ORDINARY PEOPLE'S

EXTRAORDINARY

EXPERIENCES OF THE SACRED

Northstone

Credits:
Quotation from *Denial of the Soul*
by M. Scott Peck, © 1997
by M. Scott Peck, published
by The Crown Publishing Group.

Quotations from *The Spiritual
Nature of Man: A Study of
Contemporary Religious
Experience* by Sir Alister Hardy,
1979 © 1979 Sir Alister Hardy,
used by permission of Oxford
University Press.

Quotations from Alister Hardy
Archives, used by permission of
The Alister Hardy Trust.

Quotation reprinted from *Being
Peace* (1987) by Thich Nhat Hanh
with permission of Parallax Press,
Berkeley, California.

Quotation from *The Hiding Places
of God* (1991) by John Cornwell,
used by permission of the author.

Quotations from *Exploring Inner
Space: Scientists and Religious
Experience* (1987) by David Hay,
used by permission of the author.

All quotations from the Holy
Bible are taken from the New
International Version®.
Copyright © 1973, 1978, 1984 by
International Bible Society.
Used by permission of
Zondervan Publishing House.
All rights reserved.

Editor: Michael Schwartzentruber
Proofreading: Dianne Greenslade
Cover and interior design: Margaret Kyle
Cover artwork: Lois Huey-Heck

Northstone Publishing acknowledges the financial
support of the Government of Canada, through the
Book Publishing Industry Development Program, for
its publishing activities.

Northstone Publishing is an imprint of Wood Lake Books Inc.,
an employee-owned company, and is committed to caring
for the environment and all creation. Northstone recycles,
reuses, and composts, and encourages readers to do the
same. Resources are printed on recycled paper and more
environmentally friendly groundwood papers (newsprint),
whenever possible. The trees used are replaced through
donations to the Scoutrees for Canada program.
A percentage of all profit is donated to charitable
organizations.

Canadian Cataloguing in Publication Data
Hawker, Paul, 1952-
Secret affairs of the soul
Includes bibliographical references and index.
ISBN 1-896836-42-9
1. Experience (Religion)   I. Title.
BL53.H39 2000   291.4'2 C00-910833-5

Published by Northstone Publishing,
an imprint of Wood Lake Books Inc.
Kelowna, British Columbia, Canada

Printing 10 9 8 7 6 5 4 3 2 1
Printed in Canada by Friesens

CONTENTS

PREFACE

To maintain the integrity of the accounts of the sacred and intimate experiences contained in this book, I have reproduced as accurately as possible the words and style of the language the contributors used.

As the accounts are in the respondents' own words, they will at times not fit with Northstone Publishing's house policy of using inclusive, gender neutral language when making reference to God and the Divine.

Some readers may find this difficult, but I believe it is important to allow each person who has shared their story the dignity of the language and words they themselves used so as to respect and honor their experience.

ACKNOWLEDGMENTS

My gratitude flows to all those who helped make this book possible.

Firstly to Dr. David Hay, Reader in Spiritual Education, University of Nottingham, whose work in surveying spiritual experiences was absolutely invaluable. I am totally indebted to him for generously allowing me to use material from his book *Exploring Inner Space,* thus providing a sound basis for the accounts collated in this book.

I also wish to thank the Alister Hardy Society, Oxford, England, for allowing me to use a number of accounts from their files and to also acknowledge the pioneering work Sir Alister Hardy made in the area of religious experiences.

I am extremely indebted to the Rev. Dr. Michael Mason C.SS.R. whose wonderful assistance and encouragement at the early stages of my research spurred me on. I am also thankful to him for making available accounts he received from a talk back radio program and for giving me permission to use his previously unpublished Australian survey results.

With regard to the writing and rewriting of the manuscript, I am deeply indebted to Libby Checkley for subediting many drafts before they were submitted for publication. She was a tireless sounding board for the ideas, frustrations, and breakthroughs that accompany a work such as this. Her input and enthusiastic participation was a gift I gratefully acknowledge.

My gratitude also to my wife, Christine, for her forbearance and for ensuring an appropriate perspective was maintained between the work and our lives.

Thanks also to those friends who read and offered feedback on the manuscript: Michael Adams, Dean Drayton, Rhonda Pigott, Matthew Clarke, Lisa Mangan and Vanessa Eisenberg.

I am indebted to Mike Schwartzentruber, my editor at Northstone, and the editorial panel for their indulgence with the late delivery of the manuscript and the rough early drafts.

Last, but certainly not least, a special thanks to all those people who so generously and openly shared their stories. I am extremely humbled by the trust they showed in letting me use their treasured experiences. It has been an absolute privilege to hear such rarely divulged confidences.

WE JUST DON'T KNOW

A guy sets alone out here at night, maybe readin' books or thinkin' or stuff like that. Sometimes he gets thinkin', an' he got nothing to tell him what's so an' what ain't so. Maybe if he see somethin', he don't know whether it's right or not. He can't turn to some other guy and ast him if he sees it too. He can't tell. He got nothing to measure by. I seen things out here. I wasn't drunk. I don't know if I was asleep. If some guy was with me, he could tell me I was asleep, an' then it would be all right. But I jus' don't know.

– Itinerant farm worker Lennie, from John Steinbeck's *Of Mice and Men*.[1]

There is a lot about the spiritual we "jus' don't know." This book traverses one of the huge "don't know" areas: soul affairs – those moments in our lives when we're touched by a presence or power outside ourselves, something awesome, extraordinary and exponentially different from anything else we have ever encountered; moments and events which are difficult to describe and almost impossible to explain yet are profoundly real; experiences which are indelibly etched into our consciousness and will impact us for a lifetime.

Peppered throughout this book are dozens of anecdotal accounts illustrating the commonality and range of soul affairs. Some are centuries old; most are contemporary. I have chosen them because I believe they represent what is really happening in our spiritual lives as opposed to what religion or the media would have us believe is going on. The accounts have been gleaned through a smorgasbord of collection methods. A few are from books, some are letters sent in response to radio programs, others are experiences personally related to me. The stories are the tip of the iceberg; they reflect the experiences of millions. In frankly exposing and talking about clandestine affairs of the soul, I hope to lift the veil on the topic, take away the ignorance and embarrassment that surround such affairs, and establish a bench-mark of normality on the subject. I want to take soul affairs out of the closet!

In so doing, I am breaking some of society's strongest taboos. Much of what is printed here will be uncomfortable and extremely challenging, as many of these soul affairs defy logic. Yet as we read these accounts and see how frequently soul affairs take place, we uncover an incredible anomaly: transforming moments, peak experiences, theophanies, holy instants, soul affairs, religious experiences, soul moments, epiphanies – whatever we call them – are so unusual and so profound we assume few others have had similar experiences. However, the opposite is the case; they are widespread and common, just secret.

This book is for spiritual seekers who, because of their experiences, know rather than believe that there is something – a higher plane, a higher power, a purpose, God – that there is something intangible, indefinable, something that touches our souls in an ineffable way but that is nevertheless incredibly real. It is for ordinary people who, when seeking to fit their experiences of what they call God or a higher power into a credible framework that will withstand scrutiny, find themselves bogged down in the middle of a muddy spiritual and religious no man's land.

It is relatively early days in the exploration of contemporary Western experiential spirituality and undoubtedly in years to come a much clearer and perhaps more accurately defined picture will emerge. However, by exposing the nature and extent of soul affairs my hope is that others who have also had a passionate affair of the soul – whether it be a "celestial one-night stand" or a lifelong romance – will be made aware that they are not deranged, out of their minds, or temporarily insane, but rather that they are experiencing something common to the majority of the population. Indeed, it is more than likely we are traveling in great company, often along the same paths walked by saints, mystics, and countless millions of unintentional pilgrims.

PEARLS AND DRAGONS

I don't know Who – or what – put the question, I don't know when it was put. I don't even remember answering. But at some moment I did answer Yes to Someone – or Something – and from that hour I was certain that existence is meaningful and that, therefore, my life, in self-surrender, had a goal.

– Dag Hammarskjöld[1]

There's an old Sufi story about a young man who heard about a pearl of great price, so valuable that anyone who found it would be rich for life. However, there was much myth and rumor surrounding the existence of the pearl. Some scoffed, saying the pearl was just an old wives' tale. Others said that although they'd never seen it themselves, they'd heard enough stories from others to convince them that it existed.

So the young man set out on a quest to find the pearl. After traveling many lands and asking many wise folk, he eventually found an old woman who said the pearl was in a cave high up in the mountains.

He searched high and low for many days until he at last found the cave. There in the dark recesses was the lustrous pearl. Delighted, he strode forward to pick it up only to be confronted by a huge fire breathing dragon. As he ran for his life, the dragon's flaming breath scorched his backside.

Terrified, he returned home. He was surprised to discover that when he spoke about his adventures to others who'd also seen the pearl their descriptions of the jewel and its whereabouts differed markedly from his. *They* hadn't seen any dragon – what was he on about? Others ridiculed him, asking for proof. Some dismissed his story, saying he must have been dreaming or drunk.

Ashamed of his cowardly behavior and confused by all the conflicting accounts, he began to doubt his own memory. As time went by, he eventually gave up all thoughts of such matters. He settled down to the ways of the world, established a business, married, and raised a family.

Many decades went by. His business prospered; his children grew up and left home.

With time on his hands to contemplate, he began to wonder again about the pearl. Was it still there? Had he imagined it? Was the dragon still there?

Eventually, his curiosity got the better of him. Once again he returned to the mountain.

Filled with trepidation, he re-entered the cave. There, as before, lay the pearl, pure and glowing in the light. And there, too, was the dragon guarding it, but with one difference. It was no longer the fire breathing monster that had terrified him in his youth. Now it was just a small lizard.

Like most baby boomer children brought up in the English-speaking world, institutionalized religion was a regular part of my life. Every morning, my public state high school assembly recited the Lord's Prayer and sang an English hymn. On Sundays, my parents toddled me off to the century-old Anglican church, where I sat through some of the most boring moments of my young life. To make matters worse, my parents also had the idea that the Sabbath day should be different from the rest of the week, so I wasn't allowed to play with other kids, or, as I grew older, to do odd jobs to earn extra pocket money. Unless Dad took us fishing or on a "mystery trip" in the car, Sundays were excruciatingly monotonous and drab. These days we don't often hear the phrase a "month of wet Sundays," but when I was a youngster how well I knew the meaning of it. Stuck inside, unable to wander the hills, explore rivers and ponds, or go off on a bike ride, a wet Sunday struck dread into my heart. It was my own private hell. Those who pine nostalgically for the good old days obviously had a much better slice of the post-war decades than I ever did. Thank God for books is all I can say.

When I reached adolescence, I started to balk at the weekly trips to church, for unlike school there was no opportunity to play up or reduce the tedium by asking awkward questions or indulging in mischievous pranks. The problem wasn't so much the content; I was full of admiration for this Jesus. But the way church goers and clergy conducted themselves seemed totally at odds with his message. From the pulpit, I heard how Jesus dwelt among prostitutes and cheats, and how he didn't condemn them; that he exhorted us to love our neighbors, turn the other cheek, give to the poor, forgive and show compassion. Yet among the congregants and clergy I heard gossip and harsh judgment of outsiders, especially the current outcasts of our society – bikers and unmarried mothers, some of whom were my school friends. In my innocence, I naively pointed out such inconsistencies to my parents and for my efforts received quick and harsh retribution. I instantly knew from their tone that I'd broken into one of those adult "no go" zones and that all discussion on the topic was henceforth forbidden. Usually it was subjects like sex and girls' body parts that received such tight-lipped treatment. Perhaps their attack on me was severe because the opinions I expressed reflected truths they also perceived. In any event, as conservative churchgoers, such criticisms were too dangerous to express.

Combined with this severe roasting was my parents' insistence that I, like them, do my duty and continue attending services. Frustrated, I looked for an escape clause. I found it in hiking the Tararua mountain range near my home in Wellington, New Zealand. I judiciously timed my weekend and day trips into the nearby mountains to guarantee my arrival home was too late to attend a service. It broke the ritual and I was reprieved. My church days were over and, apart from a couple of weddings, I didn't go to another church service for 17 years.

I wasn't the only one. With the exception of those in the United States, most of my baby boomer generation left church in droves.

My self-imposed weekend exiles to the mountains exposed me to the wonder of nature in its rawest, meanest, and most beautiful. They also introduced me to human intimacy the like of which I'd never previously known. Many of my friends were also instinctively drawn to the savage environment of the mountains for despite their potential danger and unpredictable nature they offered true sanctuary. The emotional refuge more than compensated for the physical hazards. We were embraced by the ruggedness that kept so many others out. It was the place we went to when no one else would have us. Unlike home, school, and church, there were no taboo topics here, nothing we couldn't discuss, argue, and debate – politics, sex, religion, each other. All bets were off, no holds barred. I relished such freedom.

Much of our free and wide ranging discussions took place as we walked the mountain trails battling blizzards, negotiating rocky peaks, and fording flooded rivers. Accompanying our escapades was a continuous verbal free for all that often continued well into the night. Safe from the storms outside our isolated mountain huts, safe from adult disapproval, safe from the constraints of polite society, we'd talk well into the evenings, our discussions punctuated by the shared sacrament of a hot brew. The meaning of life, war, hate, conscription, politics, prejudice – anything and everything was discussed fully and passionately. Confessions of adolescent lust, frustration, and sexual awkwardness were heard, accepted, and given silent absolution. The stories swapped around dozens of fires were sometimes as profound as any parable. I celebrated our camaraderie.

There were also a few "events" for which we had no explanation.

One time, a friend and I were descending a long ridge from the tops into a narrow mountain valley. It took about three hours and as it was nearing the end of a long hard day we were pretty well done in. All the way down, we both had an uncanny sense that we were being followed. At first, we thought a deer might be following us and we backtracked to see if this was the case. Nothing. As we continued downwards the feeling persisted. Coming and going, ebbing and flowing, it was rhythmic, almost hypnotic. The afternoon was eerily silent, strange for this part of the world where a 70-kph wind is common. It was like the silence before an earthquake, when all the animals and birds go deathly quiet. The only sound was the tinkling of far off waterfalls. My dog also sensed "it." Stopping often and sniffing vigorously, he too detected something, but could pick up no scent, no sound. Mysterious.

I made no conclusion about this. Instead, I simply filed it away in the "to be revealed" basket. But this and other incidents – especially the close calls, near misses, and brushes with death – served to dislodge my certainty. So too did the occasional moments of beauty so breathtakingly stunning we could only stand and admire in silent awe.

One evening in particular stands out. We'd climbed in thick cloud all day and had finally reached the alpine hut that was our overnight destination. While my friend cooked the evening meal, I glanced outside. Seeing a break in the clouds, I thought there might be the chance of a view. I wandered down the slope to a lookout point where I could see over the cliff edge. There I stood and watched.

The mountain I was standing on was completely surrounded by a plain of fluffy, corrugated clouds stretching dozens of kilometers off into the distance. Above and beyond was clear, but all below was obscured by the cloud that started about 50 meters or so beneath me. Standing on the edge of the precipice, I had no land reference points. It was as if I was standing on the clouds themselves, an angel in heaven. I watched the setting sun cast colors onto my clouds – pinks, then golds with purples out on the far edges. It was so beautiful I held my breath so as to capture the consummate peace of this exquisite moment.

There was no great voice, no burning bush, but internally something "clicked." I had a deep, clear sense, a fragment of awareness, that all before me had been created, and that this creation somehow accommodated me. I too was part of it. The essence that had brought all this into being also included me. I, what lay before me, and its creator, were part of the same entity. A warm feeling grew inside me, a knowing that I was *enjoyed* as much as I was *enjoying* the moment. It is as clear to me now as it was all those decades ago.

I lingered a few moments longer and then, somewhat incredulous, returned to the hut. I knew the moment had been very special. I had been touched by something that was much more than a great view. It was deeper and more encompassing than anything I had ever encountered. Having no framework or concept to hang this experience on, and no language to express it, I kept it to myself. I had no idea it was a common moment of transcendence, an affair of the soul.

I was deeply touched by this experience. It was far less de-fined but much more real than anything I had encountered within the four walls of a church. Indeed, so different was it from my experience of organized religion that I didn't recognize this expe-rience as having anything to do with God. I also had no idea that in the honest, open, and accepting community I shared with my companions we were being Christ to each other, for it too was light years away from my experience of the religion of Christ.

Running away from my religious dragon catapulted me into a non-religious world. I lived the next couple of decades as an ordinary citizen, unaware that my exposure to religion at a young age had given me a concept and yearning for God. The problem was that with no belief or faith in religious institutions, I assumed I had no legitimate way of connecting with the divine. I was spiri-tually homeless. Not that I knew any of this at the time. Such thoughts hardly entered my mind as I lived life to the full. But things have a habit of catching up with us.

CHAPTER TWO

RETURNING TO THE CAVE

The most beautiful emotion we can experience is the mystical. It is the power of all true art and science. He to whom this emotion is a stranger, who can no longer wonder and stand rapt in awe, is as good as dead. To know that what is impenetrable to us really exists, manifesting itself as the highest wisdom and the most radiant beauty, which our dull faculties can comprehend only in their most primitive forms – this knowledge, this feeling, is at the center of true religiousness. In this sense, and in this sense only, I belong to the rank of devoutly religious men.

– Albert Einstein[1]

Like most men in their 40s, I have had many adventures, fallen in love more than once, married, had children, worked a couple of careers, and bought a few houses. My wife, Christine, and I earn our living making documentaries and commercial films for television and private clients. It's a job I enjoy immensely and it has enabled me to live a very privileged lifestyle traveling the world and meeting people from all walks of life. By our culture's standards, we'll never be rich, but as we've always valued lifestyle over wealth, we're very happy with our lot. Although we've met with the occasional crisis, our family has been blessedly free of tragedy. I am keenly aware that all this could change in an instant, but until it does I'm grateful for the wonderful life we've led. No grievous accidents, no disease or lingering illness, no sudden deaths – we have been very fortunate. I am like so many others in the First World – a very ordinary, if somewhat lucky man.

However, like the young man in the Sufi story, I eventually reached a stage in my life where I was happily married, my children had grown up, and my business had prospered. Everything our culture claimed was necessary for comfort and well-being I now had. I should have been content and happy, yet the very opposite was the case. Something was missing. Something indefinable. The feeling had begun in my late 20s and intensified throughout my 30s. I read books, attended courses, sought counseling and plagued my friends with meaning-of-life type questions. My search even led me back to institutionalized religion which, although giving me a few tools and some glimpses of God, failed to deliver what I was looking for. I was a lost soul searching for meaning. Exactly what I was looking for I didn't know; I just knew I hadn't found it yet. I felt alone, hollow, and a fraud. There was a hole in my soul and I yearned for it to be filled.

It seemed I had done everything I could possibly do and had almost reached a stage of desperation when a chance conversation with an old friend changed everything. I was telling him that I felt as if I were drifting rudderless through life. Life had turned out far better than I had expected. So why was I so melancholy? Why plagued by this grief that had no reason?

"Sounds like you need a wilderness experience, mate: 40 days and 40 nights."

He even named the site for my sojourn – a small cabin high in the isolated mountains where I had spent so much of my youth. There I could seek in solitude what I couldn't find in society. He watered a seed that had lain dormant for a very long time. So I announced to my wife, Christine, my intention to live almost six weeks in solitude and she, used to my occasional life lurches, helped me buy the necessary alpine equipment, board a plane, and head back to New Zealand.

It was quite an adventure, to say the least. My soul was touched in places I never knew existed. But there was one experience in particular that had an immense impact on me, an event so profound and beyond all my decades of experience on this planet that my view of God, life, and spirituality was irrevocably changed.

On the tenth morning of my self-imposed exile, I woke up with a definite thought or yearning or unspoken suggestion to go up onto the ridge behind the small cabin where I was overnighting. Perhaps it was only an impulse. I don't really know. Being on my own, I had gradually become used to hearing an "inner voice" and was acting on it much more than I normally would have in my day-to-day life surrounded by the busyness of friends, family, and colleagues.

I was disinclined to get out of my warm sleeping bag because it was a particularly cold morning – icicles were dripping from the cabin roof – but the small quiet "voice" was so clear and it resonated so well that I finally donned my stormproof mountain clothing and wandered up to the ridge.

When I reached the top, I sat down and began to gaze into the steep mountain valley that stretched out below. Instantly, my awareness changed. Without any thinking or effort on my part, suddenly I was conscious in a radically different way. It felt like I had been plugged in to the mainframe of the universe and was directly connected to an inexplicable and incomprehensibly vast form of otherness – the "Source" of it all.

As I gazed down into the distant river valleys, they took on a clarity and vibrancy I had never before experienced. Everything around me was so crisp and clear, really and fully alive. It was as if I had spent my life wandering around in a fog and suddenly it had lifted. It was one of the clearest, most real moments of my life.

I was totally transported and cocooned – mesmerized by the profundity of it all. I had encountered nothing previously in my life as powerful as this. Even the surges of passionate romantic love or the chemically-induced highs I had experienced seemed trite in comparison. This was no revelation gleaned by my own thinking, the result of an intellectual logical process, or months of pondering and effort. I had been given a gift, a "knowing." This gift seemed to come both from within and from outside of me – so vast it transcended time boundaries, yet solid and rooted to all that was and ever would be. My emotional reference points no longer applied.

I wasn't overwhelmed or frightened, for combined with this "knowing" was an intense and unquenchable sense of support. It mattered not what I did, where I went, or who I was, because I, too, was an integral part of this Source. I sensed no separation between it, me, and anything else. I was an undiminished and complete part of it, as much as the mountains, plants, air, and the water that inexorably flowed in the streams. We, it, I, them, the Source – all were beautifully and totally interwoven with each other, constantly evolving, yet perfect at every stage and in every shape and form. I felt humbled and privileged, yet worthy of it, all at once. I sensed, too, that this was no final definition. On the contrary, what had been revealed was but one drop in the ocean of an awesome and unfathomable concept.

The whole experience felt like hours, yet I knew it had only been a few minutes. When it finally dissolved away, I was left slightly incredulous as to whether it had actually happened. But the warmth and support of that moment remained. It stayed with me the rest of that day and throughout the ensuing days, weeks, months, and years. It's still with me today. Like a glowing coal, it sits there deeply embedded in my soul, in the furthest reaches of my inner being. I suspect it will never leave.

I had been given the pearl of great price – a gift that I recognized. Now that I was older and wiser I wasn't going to give it up easily.

As the remaining weeks of solitude unfolded, there were other great moments. Some with as much impact as the one I've just described. Together they formed a spiritual critical mass which, when I emerged from the mountains, I was bursting to tell. The problem was I found it extremely difficult to communicate what I had experienced.

When talking about my experiences, the only way I could even begin to describe them was to say that they were better than sex. I would then jokingly add that that either showed how good they were, or how bad my sex life was! But no other metaphor seemed to describe what it was like. No other experience had had such intensity, such power to overwhelm me, or the potency to totally focus me, yet transport me out of myself. In all my decades, nothing had been better than those moments on the mountain. Nothing else had ever made me feel so alive, so good, so complete, so integrated, so whole. "Soul orgasm" or "soul sex" was the only way I could think of describing it.

But no matter how I described it, how many metaphors I invented, nothing seemed to suffice. I would leave each conversation frustrated that there was so much left unsaid, so much more to tell, and I had to tell it. I would have exploded if I didn't! So I began to write. I wrote and re-wrote until I was satisfied I had an honest account of how it really was. The result was *Soul Survivor: A Spiritual Quest Through 40 Days and 40 Nights of Mountain Solitude* (Northstone, 1998).

The book is a love story. A bodice ripping, passionate and tumultuous love affair of the soul. A warts-and-all account of a soul's wooing, seduction, and consummation with its "Own One," the Source, God.

After writing the book, I was curious to know how many others might have had experiences similar to mine. After all, I was just an ordinary guy who'd had an extra-ordinary experience – there must be others like me. Yet finding them proved to be a frustrating task. It was such a vague topic. What do you call such moments?

I started with "religious experience" and began plowing through public and theological libraries. However, "religious experience" was a confusing term because it tended to exclude those who didn't consider themselves particularly pious or devout – that is, most people. So I widened my search to the Internet using keyword combinations of "ecstatic," "mystical," "transcendent," "holy," and "sacred." A "sacred transformations" site produced some results that seemed to fit the picture, but it was a grab bag collection of near-death experiences, angel visitations, mystical moments, and the like. Unfortunately, as with many Internet websites, the lack of a screening process meant that along with the authentic experiences were many that were clearly the writings of psychiatrically disturbed or drug-affected individuals. Was I in the same category as some of these clearly deranged folk? Where were "normal" people like me? It was starting to become a bit of a worry!

I kept looking because deep down I really believed I wasn't alone. I had always suspected that most Westerners have a much deeper spirituality than they're credited with. Besides, I simply couldn't believe that experiences of such magnitude could happen to someone as ordinary as me and not to anyone else.

I kept searching. This time through encyclopedias, books, and journals. To my amazement, I discovered my experience tallied with those of the mystics.

The highest stage of union is an indescribable experience, in which all idea of images and forms and differences has vanished. All consciousness of self and of all things has gone and the soul is plunged into the abyss of the Godhead and the spirit has become one with God.

– Suso, German 14th-century mystic[2]

I also discovered that my quip that what I had experienced in the mountains was better than sex seemed to have some substance. Many mystics speak of, and seek, erotic and spiritual dissolution of their "self" into the divine "Other." One authority on the subject suggested that the ability to relinquish control through the loss of physical and psychological boundaries is similar in both the profound experiences of sex and mysticism.[3]

I could certainly relate to this! My mountain experiences were very much like but much better than sex, because they were the first time I'd ever had a total union of my mind and soul with another. This would never be achievable with another human being no matter how compatible or how good a lover they were. We would never "know" each other the way I knew and was known by the Source, the All.

I identified so strongly with the descriptions of the mystical union that I began to think I might perhaps be a mystic. I pushed this one away as in my experience those who make such self-proclamations are all too often fraudulent posers. Besides, I didn't fit the job description. It appeared most who gained the lofty mystical heights spent years, even decades, in meditation, prayer, solitude, fasting, studying and/or being in a cloistered religious order – none of which I had done. Many had also lived lives of incredible suffering and had died horrible deaths. There was no way I was in this league and I didn't want to be either. I was quite happy being an ordinary guy. I was loud, irreverent and brash, and enjoyed living life to the full, especially when fooling about with my sons. Perhaps I had experienced a mystical moment, but that alone didn't make me a mystic. That path required much more than the spiritual one-night stands I had enjoyed on occasion.

One thing I did notice, however, was that, like me, the mystics had incredible difficulty expressing what they had experienced. If experts had such trouble, what hope was there for the rest of us? Perhaps accounts from ordinary folks were so few and far between not because we don't have soul affairs, but because they are so difficult to describe.

CHAPTER THREE

EXPRESSING THE INEXPRESSIBLE

Our true history is scarcely ever deciphered by others. The chief part of the drama is a monologue, or rather an intimate debate between God, our conscience, and ourselves. Tears, griefs, depressions, disappointments, irritations, good and evil thoughts, decisions, uncertainties, deliberations – all these belong to our secret, and are almost all incommunicable and intransmissible, even when we try to speak of them, and even when we write them down.

– Henri-Frédéric Amiel[1]

Who can describe the wonder felt when gazing at a newborn baby? Who can put into words the splendor of standing on a beach at dawn and watching the sun rise? Who can convey the experience of seeing, for the first time, a stiff, cold body laid out in a coffin?

Imagine trying to explain orgasm to someone who has never had one. Think of the difficulty, the incomprehensibility, the lack of common reference points with which to communicate any meaning. Suppose you've just fallen head over heels in love with the man or woman of your dreams. How can you explain what's happening to someone who has never been similarly smitten?

How can you prove this love you experience is a real and tangible thing, not something you made up?

When it comes to human feelings and emotions, there are experiences so profound and so precious we could never explain them even if we wanted to. No matter what words, what logic or proofs we use, there is no way they can ever be fully understood until they are experienced. They are inexpressible. It is this ineffability that keeps our soul affairs secret. In my search for other people's soul affairs I came across many folk who, like me, struggled to put their experience into words.

It affects me physically. When I look back on the event, I'm instantly there again and I get this funny feeling in my stomach – sort of queasy. It's really strong, a nervous, excited feeling, like when you're about to embark on something unknown. Not scared, just excited. I even remember the smell. It's really hard to describe. All of a sudden it just floods back to me and I'm aware of it all again. The feeling has never left me.

I was on holiday. We had arrived the night before in a new city and for some reason I woke up at 4:30 that morning. The sun was shining through the open window and there was a slight breeze blowing through too. All of a sudden, I just knew that everything was perfect. I lay there and let the smell surround me. I felt the warmth of the sun. It was wonderful.

The feeling continued for the rest of the day. It was like I wasn't in my body. I did the normal routines, but it was like I was lumping around this big physical mass that was sort of unnecessary. It was just so perfect, so peaceful. I could have coped with anything that day. It was as if nothing could upset me or affect me. It was the weirdest feeling.

I wasn't stressed or pressured or anything. It just came out of the blue. Even when we walked across the oval to the supermarket, the breeze seemed to emphasize the harmony I felt.

I don't really know what it was; I just wish it would happen again! I think that there is something "out there" and that there's hope. It definitely gives me hope. Since then I'm no longer afraid of dying. Not that I'd throw myself under a bus or anything, but maybe the next step when we die is some sort of eternal perfection like what I experienced on that day. It certainly feels right.

I don't need explanations or reasons for what happened. I'm quite happy living the rest of my life wondering about it and I'm content that other people are wondering the same things. I'd rather do that than categorize it or give it a reason that I can't back up, like you have to do with religion. My religion is believing what I know is true, what I've experienced. I can't believe in something that I don't know. It was just a gift I was given from somewhere; I don't know from where. I'm not special or singled out in getting it – just lucky.

I wouldn't say it was God as God's been described to me, or what I was told was God when I was growing up. I went to a Catholic primary school for a couple of years and we were told to pray and to sing songs to this God/person/thing – somebody I didn't know or understand, somebody no one even seemed interested in explaining to me.

I believe there's obviously something going on out there, some "otherness," and we don't know what it is. It just blows me away. Who made me? Where do we come from? The mind that was put with our bodies is amazing, but the knowledge we have of otherness is so limited really. Maybe we're just part of some big experiment? With people dying of cancer and wars and things, it's almost as if something, someone, somewhere, some consciousness, is sitting back thinking, where did I go wrong?

I'm changed because I have things in a bigger perspective. Things like my makeup being wrong or what other people think of me used to worry me. Now I remember that day and I realize it's not all that important. It's not so bad when things go wrong. Now when I get a bit down, I just think back and I know that there's a "perfection" or something out there that I can tap into.

— Female secretary aged 21*

It happened to me at the age of about four years, before any knowledge of any religions or of any gods.

My family and an uncle's family went for a picnic. Somehow, I went for a walk on my own. I found a hill covered with bracken and I walked up to it. I had to use an almost swimming motion to part the bracken. I must have been small, because I needed to jump up now and then to see where I was.

Eventually, I came to a fence which I could not get beyond, so I stood and leaned against it. I could see the hill I was on, and on the other side was a hill covered with trees. The bracken was moving in the breeze, flowing like water back and forth, and I became lost. People these days would say that the "I" became lost. I was part of it all and it was part of me. A sense of union, a sense of being beyond words. I do not know how to put it into words. A sense of knowing? And awareness of…?

How long I was there I do not know. Eventually I got back to the families and they were sitting having lunch. They asked where I had been, and I told them that I had been for a walk. Then they wanted to know what I had been doing and I tried to tell them.

Everybody laughed. That is what changed my life.

---

* All accounts not attributed to other published sources are from the author's collection.

I clammed up from then on. Until… But that is another long story. Much agony. But the few times of ecstasy keep one going. The mystic awareness has never left me, but there were times when I left it. But have come back to it.

There have been many knowings since. I am now just a few months off 70 years of age, and I am thankful that I have read not only William James' *Varieties of Religious Experience* but also William Sargent's *Battle for the Mind*.

None of my experience has turned me to religion. And yet I recognize the power of prayer. And the only prayer I can make is that advised in *The Cloud of Unknowing*. I am not a Christian. Although they tried to make a Christian out of me, it did not take. I have no religion, but this does not make me an atheist. And I am not so bold as to call myself a gnostic, but this does not make me agnostic. If I name it, I limit it to the concept that name implies. It is vaster than any name.

I am tempted to say it, so I will say it. The only thing that makes sense is paradox. The single rose is now the garden.

— Man early 70s

Here are two people at vastly different stages of life, both struggling to put into words their experience. In trying to explain the inexplicable to others, the boy encountered ridicule ensuring his soul affairs remained secret throughout his lifetime. The young woman had also kept her experience to herself, not because she feared ridicule, but, as she later explained, because of a frustrating inability to adequately convey what had occurred. These are not isolated cases. In struggling to express our experiences, at best, all we can do is give an approximation of our encounter.

In addition to the inadequacies of language, there are other factors that inhibit us from talking about our soul affairs. In our society, it is inappropriate to divulge the intimacies of our sexual encounters to an undiscerning general audience, for such moments are sacred, not ones to be betrayed through careless banter. The same is true for our intimate spiritual experiences. That these moments are often intangible adds to their sacredness. To confide an intimate experience to someone and to be misunderstood would almost certainly sully the experience, perhaps destroying the precious intimacy that existed. We don't put our pillow talk out for the world to probe and comment on and for the same reason this, our private spiritual pillow talk, often stays with us to the grave.

Yet it goes further than this, for unlike the way we might hint at other profound or intimate moments in our lives we seldom allude to our soul affairs. After all, who can we tell? Where is a suitable forum for airing such experiences? Even our life partners may not understand.

I've told very few people about these events in the way I'm describing them now. It's too hard and I doubt many would understand.

It happened about seven years ago. I'd got up early, gone for a run along the beach, worked at my job for a few hours, then sat with accountants and solicitors for the remainder of the day, listening to the stark reality of the state of my affairs. It's safe to say I was stressed at the time. Lost and fearful. Heavily burdened. I felt very much alone.

I had an evening meeting to attend in the club rooms of the sporting oval, but as there was an hour or two before it started I parked the car near the sports grounds and decided to just walk around for a while.

As I strolled past the gates of the oval, I was suddenly overcome by a feeling of well-being – quite a contrast from my feelings moments earlier. The place took on a warmth and a brightness. I was almost at one with myself. I felt as if I had no cares at all in the world (and boy, my life was the opposite to that). It was a moment of absolute bliss. It's hard to describe really. Just a feeling of total support and comfort and well-being. I felt as if someone was with me, and that I was to be looked after.

Eventually, when it came time for the meeting, the first stranger I met, I felt a complete benevolence towards them.

I call my time in the park my "spiritual awakening." I now know that there is a higher power – whatever it is, whatever you want to call it – that loves me and is interested in my welfare. It wouldn't surprise me if this higher power could be the same one that's worshipped in the religions – Buddhist, Christian, whatever. I just know what I experienced. It doesn't really worry me all that much what label is put on it.

The only time I can recall feeling this way before, was as a carefree child skipping through the green English meadows of my childhood.

Today I do sometimes ponder over that day in the park, and how it felt, and I do believe I can feel that again. Sometimes I think that is how some people feel most of the time. Was it possible that day that I felt for the first time in my life that I was loved?

– Businessman aged 38

The above anecdotes are not from transcendental meditators, or people who consider themselves mystics or deeply religious. They are from ordinary, everyday Westerners. These are their priceless pearls. They are a random selection from my own collected accounts and are representative of a common occurrence. I can say this with confidence because after many months of searching, I finally found authoritative proof that my hunches were right. I definitely was not alone in having had a sensuous affair of the soul.

In a study done by the Religious Experience Unit, Oxford University, England, were thousands of accounts of profound affairs of the soul – the religious and spiritual experiences of people of all ages, from all walks of life: devout and secular, young and old, rich and poor. Ordinary people like me. What made these accounts so different from other forays into the topic was that here there was no attempt by the researchers to interpret or analyze individual soul affairs. Rather, their mission was simply to collate accounts to show their frequency, type, and range.

Surprisingly, the Oxford study on the spiritual/religious nature of Westerners wasn't done by theologians, philosophers, religious scholars, or the church. Instead, it was undertaken by scholars completely outside the humanities – biologists no less! Due to the compartmentalizing of academic research, their scientific study seldom made it onto the radar screens of social scientists and herein lay the reason for my difficulty in accessing it.

It's ironic that this incredibly important spiritual research was initiated by hard scientists who are seen as the traditional opponents of religion and spirituality. But what's more astonishing is that even though the studies shattered myths and revealed levels of spiritual experiences far beyond what would be expected in a secular rational society, the findings have been virtually ignored. It seems that this is one area of knowledge we just don't want to know about. It's as if we're ashamed to admit that we who live in such an enlightened age of reason can at the same time experience such irrational and illogical encounters of God or a higher power.

CHAPTER FOUR

RESEARCH RESULTS

We must conclude that it is not only a particular political ideology that has failed, but the idea that men and women could ever define themselves in terms that exclude their spiritual needs.

– Salman Rushdie[1]

Sir Alister Hardy (1896–1985) was a distinguished ocean biologist. Beginning in the 1920s, he pioneered methods of monitoring plankton, the small marine organisms that are the base of the ocean food chain. He designed and built the Hardy Continuous Plankton Recorder which, when towed for long distances behind ships, captures random samples of plankton on a continuous roll of fine silk. The simplicity of the device allows sailors on merchant ships to use it easily and, since coming into service, more than four million miles of ocean have been tested and a plankton database of around 200,000 samples has been analyzed. This information has proven invaluable, not only in measuring changes in fish stocks but also in providing an extensive historical reference of the condition of the ocean from which the effects of pollution, exploitation, and climate change can be measured.

However, Hardy was more than a scientist. He was a painter of considerable ability and he also had a lifelong fascination for what he called "man's transcendental experiences." They so intrigued him that from the age of 30 he collected firsthand accounts such as this one.

—●—

One day as I was walking along Marylebone Road I was suddenly seized with an extraordinary sense of great joy and exaltation, as though a marvellous beam of spiritual power had shot through me linking me in a rapture with the world, the Universe, Life with a capital L, and all the beings around me. All delight and power, all things living, all time fused in a brief second.[2]

Hardy regarded the collection of such accounts as being an important part of a rounded biological perspective. He argued that one of the greatest contributions biology could make to the world would be "to work out an ecological outlook that took into account not only man's economic and nutritional needs but also his emotional and spiritual behaviour."[3] It seems Hardy was either decades ahead of his time or a remarkably balanced scientist, for at the time he expressed these notions biology was hardly a discipline noted for embracing mystery, religion, and spirituality. Quite the opposite in fact.

Hardy pointed out that since a dimension of spiritual awareness and religiosity appeared to be universal to all humans from both primitive and sophisticated cultures, we should be much better informed about our own culture's experience of spirituality. Extensive anthropological studies of indigenous cultures meant far more was known about the nature and extent of their religious practices than about our own. In Western countries, although there was a wealth of material published by institutional religion about itself and its beliefs, there was very little on the private spiritual and religious experiences of ordinary people. Recognizing this intellectual vacuum, Hardy raised funds at the end of his biology career to pursue such studies and in 1968 established the Religious Experience Research Unit at Oxford University, England.

Being a biologist rather than a theologian, Hardy was not concerned with verifying what people had experienced, but simply wished to collect "specimens" (accounts of experiences) which could then be collated and classified. As he pointed out, although science itself could never deal with the real essence of the nature of art or poetry or our innate sense of curiosity and love of adventure, it would never deny such things existed. He argued that science has to recognize that people have a spiritual side to their nature and that what was needed was "to present such a weight of *objective* evidence in the form of *written records* of these subjective spiritual feelings and of their effects on the lives of the people concerned, that the intellectual world must come to see that they are in fact as real and as influential as are the forces of love."[4] [Hardy's italics]

At no stage was it the unit's intention to scientifically "prove" that God did or did not exist or to find support for any religious doctrine or practices. Hardy just wanted evidence of what was occurring within his own culture.

To gather accounts of religious and spiritual experiences, the unit first advertised in religious magazines inviting people to write in telling of their encounters. The response was disappointingly small. Publicizing the program in the secular press and distributing pamphlets to the general population produced a much better result. Eventually more than 3,000 letters came in. The unit has continued to collect such accounts to the present day and the archive now holds approximately 6,000 such anecdotes.

In the same way botanic or biological specimens are classified, from the first 3,000 accounts 12 categories and 109 subcategories were drawn up. It is beyond the scope of this book to explore the classifications in detail, but what immediately struck me was how comparatively few accounts were of the sort popularly described as spiritual experiences. Things such as extrasensory perception, déjà vu, hearing voices, supposed contact with the dead, out of body experiences, speaking in tongues (ancient languages), being healed, telepathy, clairvoyance, and apparitions were mentioned by less than 8% of the respondents. Yet these would be the ones we would most likely find in the popular press.

Hardy's letters overwhelmingly contained experiences that recorded such things as a sense of ecstasy, guidance, inspiration, prayers answered, peace, joy, clarity, certainty, enlightenment, visions, a sense of well-being, God and/or an impression of a non-human presence: experiences that in the public's perception would be considered extremely rare or restricted to a religious minority. Here are a few examples to show the range and nature of the letters.

I heard nothing, yet it was as if I were surrounded by golden light and as if I only had to reach out my hand to touch God himself who was so surrounding me with his compassion.[5]

— Unidentified respondent

I find it difficult to describe my experience, only to say that it seems to be outside of me and enormous and yet at the same time I am part of it, everything is. It is purely personal and helps me to live and to love others. It is difficult to describe, but in some way because of this feeling I feel united to all people, to all living things. Of recent years the feeling has become so strong that I am now training to become a social worker because I find that I must help people: in some way I feel their unhappiness as my own.

– Unidentified respondent (663)

When I was on holiday, aged about 17, I glanced down and watched an ant striving to drag a bit of twig through a patch of sun on a wall in the graveyard of a Greek church, while chanting came from within the white building. The feeling aroused in me was quite unanticipated, welling up from some great depth, and essentially timeless. The concentration of simplicity and innocence was intensely of some vital present. I've had similar experiences on buses, suddenly watching people and being aware how right everything essentially is.

– Unidentified respondent (680)

When I was about 8 years old, we were living in the country. At the foot of our garden was a very old large pear tree, which at the time was crammed with white blossom and at its summit a blackbird was singing, while beyond the tree a meadow sloped up to a marvellous sunrise. As I looked at this someone or something said to me: "That is beautiful," and immediately the whole scene lit up as though a bright light had been turned on, irradiating everything. The meadow was a more vivid green, the pear tree glowed and the blackbird's song was more loud and sweet. A curious thrill ran down my spine.

– Man aged 78 (98)

I cannot say how long it took to develop, but the ecstasy lasted over roughly three weeks. The main sensation was of being loved, a flood of sweetness of great strength, without any element of sentimentality or anything but itself. The description is quite inadequate. I also felt a unification of myself with the external world: I did not lose my own identity, yet all things and I somehow entered into each other; all things seemed to "speak" to me. Something was communicated to me, not in words or images, but in another form of knowing.

– Man aged 47 (793)

The response to prayer has seemed dramatic, in that I have received an almost physical sense of comfort in times of great stress…There have been times when I have not been able to pray –this I cannot explain – but when I did so – even in the most tentative and imperfect way – the response was there, and this is a humbling thought… All I can say is that I know in my essential being that the power is there, and I have over many years had ample proof of it. [6]

– Unidentified respondent

In August last year I had what I think can only be described as a religious experience. I was recovering from a very distressing love affair and was staying with some friends and their children at a beach cottage. The wife had, some months previously in London, introduced me to a book on Chinese philosophy, the *I Ching*, and although it quite impressed me at the time I did not give much more thought to it in my preoccupations. Quite by chance – how important and strange that factor is – someone else gave me a copy of the very same book, just as I was about to leave for my holiday. When I arrived I started to read it in detail and I began to be aware of a feeling that I was about to grasp something terribly important. I was terrified to speak about it in case the feeling left me before I had properly grasped what it was about. For the next few days, I gave the book my undivided attention and gradually I became aware that I had an explanation for the previously inexplicable, that there was an order in the intangible world of emotions, relationships, and "happenings" which followed a similar kind of order to things in the physical world. I realised that the natural (the nurturing of each in reference to the other) could produce harmony of being, or "serenity" if you like, and that God was overseer of this. This insight made Christianity comprehensible to me and I realised that contact with God had to be reinforced and strengthened, as it was vital to achieving the desired harmony. The ritual of religion now had a meaning which is why I decided to go regularly to church [Church of England].

– Female aged 54 (2269)

These letters served to refute the commonly held view that unless you put in the hard yards of prayer and penance you wouldn't be rewarded with religious, mystical, or ecstatic moments. That a religious experience might occur spontaneously to ordinary people was considered to be unlikely. Hardy's letters contradicted this notion. These people weren't seeking a "religious" experience – it was something that just happened.

However, as interesting as the letters were, it was not possible to know from them how common or widespread such spiritual experiences were. Did such things happen across the whole popu-lation or only to those who were naturally mystical or religious? To find out, Hardy invited David Hay to join the unit. Hay, a zo-ologist at Nottingham University, had been exploring the area of religious experience with some of his students.

In 1976, the first national survey of religious experience in Great Britain was undertaken. A sample of the general popula-tion was asked the following question: "Have you ever been aware of, or influenced by, a presence or power, whether you call it God or not, which is different from your everyday self?" This and other questions were inserted into nationwide opinion polls. When the results were compiled, the researchers were quite surprised.

In 1965, approximately 10–15% of the British population regu-larly attended church, so it was expected a smaller percentage than this might answer "yes" to the question. At this stage, they also thought it would most likely be "religious" folk who went to church who would report such experiences.

But the survey showed that powerful spiritual experiences were reported by almost three times as many as those who went to church: 36% (41% of women and 31% of men).[7] When a follow-up Gallup poll was undertaken in 1985 by the Alister Hardy Research Centre, the figures had only dropped slightly, to 33%. On this basis it could be assumed that approximately 15 million British adults had had a profound spiritual experience!

Their curiosity aroused by the high reporting rate, David Hay's Nottingham research team selected a random sample of local people and, armed with a 27-page questionnaire, set off to interview them in their own homes.

Nottingham was not noted for fervent religious outpourings, so it wasn't expected that this door-to-door survey would produce much higher results than those of the national poll, but it did. Nearly two-thirds (62%)[8] of the respondents, almost double that of the national poll, not only affirmed they had had an experience, but also described it in detail. Why the extraordinarily different results? Had the researchers chosen a biased sample? Were people giving answers just to please the interviewer, bending the truth a little?

To ensure this wasn't the case, Hay's team built into the questionnaire "social desirability indicators," questions to judge how candid the interviewee was being. The average score for those who reported experiences was lower on these indicators than for those not reporting. This meant the replies they were getting were more genuine and honest than those of non-reporters! But why were there so many accounts, compared to the national poll?

The Nottingham researchers concluded it was due to the exceptionally conducive conditions established during the long interviews. Compared to most opinion pollsters who have limited time and a range of topics to canvas, Hay's team had only one topic and spent about an hour with each person in their own home. This built up a trusting relationship that overcame people's natural reticence to talk about such matters. Thus, far more revealing answers were offered.

I had often encountered this phenomenon while conducting my own professional television interviews. In the same way that medical specialists are given license to probe body parts usually considered off limits, documentary interviewers like myself are frequently given liberty to probe the intimacies of inner lives. Once permission is given for a personal, telephone, or on-camera interview to take place, one of the key barriers to interpersonal privacy drops away. By sensitively inviting interviewees to examine their lives, I have been privileged to hear many intimate disclosures.

One time, I was working on a health commercial, filming a businessman as he went through his day. Filming had gone smoothly; we'd done a few interviews and shot a few sequences of him at work. We were waiting for the light to be right for the final scene – a run along the beach at sunset. We had an hour or so before dusk so we sat and talked. By this stage I knew far more about him than he did about me so I took the opportunity to explore some common ground. He had been a top executive with a young and aggressive company that had gone into receivership the year before. Since then he had had long spells of unemployment which caused him to undertake some deep soul searching. As the conversation gradually became more intimate, we exchanged confidences about our lives and our sense of meaning and purpose.

We got on to the topic of spirituality and I discovered that although he had been raised Catholic, apart from the odd wedding and funeral, he had not been to church since he was 17. He certainly wouldn't have described himself as religious. Even so, he seemed to be no stranger to spiritual matters and was comfortable talking about the subject – not what I would normally expect from a high-flying businessman. I sensed that somehow he knew about "otherness" and intimate affairs of the soul. I was right. We became friends and a while later he told me the story I included in the previous chapter: the account of the late afternoon in the park.

When done benevolently, documentary filmmakers conduct interviews in an almost optimum set of conditions under which people will divulge innermost feelings and thoughts they have rarely spoken of before. Often unintentionally, we wander into natural forums for the exchange of truth – deep heart truth, the essence of our souls. When you're in that territory, it doesn't matter what the topic is or who is talking; it's a whole different world. As novelist Shirley Hazzard puts it, "I cannot tell you what truth is – except that we know it when we hear it; and that telling it without animus rancor, gives a pleasure unlike any other."[9]

During many of my conversations, people would tell me that they had never shared such personal information with anyone else. Others would joke that they felt like they were in the confessional. They were right. Sometimes I heard sorrows and regrets that were deeply buried festering sores. Somehow, as an interested and considerate stranger, I was trusted with their confidences, even more than their friends and family – perhaps even more so than their counselors. I was just like them, a struggling human being, a very open listener with no axe to grind or judgment to make. Like the Nottingham researchers, I simply wanted them to tell their story and I tried to make this as easy as possible for them.

Some people experience this on long international flights. They sit next to a complete stranger and by the end of the trip it's as if they've known each other for years. The circumstances often determine this. It is so rare to have the time to listen, and rarer still to be listened to.

As the Nottingham researchers discovered, given the right questions and an empathetic ear, ordinary people will disclose spiritual experiences of an incredibly intimate nature. The frank and open-hearted responses that David Hay's team recorded during their door-to-door survey led them to believe that with differently worded questions, and a more thorough challenging of those who may have forgotten or chosen to dismiss their spiritual experiences, they might have achieved even higher reporting rates than the 62% "yes" response they obtained. This was a conclusion Abraham Maslow, the famous American psychologist, had come to a decade earlier.

CHAPTER FIVE

PEAKS AND PRIVATE RELIGION

When a man follows the way of the world, or the way of the flesh, or the way of tradition (i.e. when he believes in religious rites and the letter of the Scriptures, as though they were intrinsically sacred), knowledge of Reality cannot arise in him.

– Shankara (9th century CE)[1]

Abraham Maslow (1908–1970) was a founder of humanist psychology and did much of the groundwork for our modern management models. He approached psychology from a different perspective than his famous predecessors, Freud and Jung. "I was awfully curious to find out why I didn't go insane," he once said. He studied the psychology of well-being, of well-adjusted people, and from this deduced his well-known personality development theory based on a hierarchy of needs.

Maslow saw human needs as a pyramid. At the base of the pyramid are our essential physical needs – water, food, air, and sex. These needs are our strongest motivators. No one worries too much about the meaning of life when they are starving to death. The next level up on the pyramid is our desire and need for safety. Physical security, stability, freedom from illness, anxiety, and danger are just a few of the things we seek. Those who don't have these basic needs met as children develop anxiety and neurosis in adulthood. Maslow stated that unfulfilled needs at this lower level of the pyramid would prohibit a person from climbing to the next step.

Next come the social and psychological needs: the need for love, friendship, a mate, a family, and the need to belong to a club, nation, or neighborhood. Many people remain stuck at this stage, constantly looking for love and acceptance. Only by receiving adequate love can a person continue to develop and move to the next level.

Esteem needs come next. Maslow defined two levels of esteem needs: self-esteem and reputation. Self-esteem is a person's own feelings of worth and confidence, whereas reputation is based on recognition and prestige reflecting other people's opinions. Interestingly enough, self-esteem is more important to most people than how they are perceived by others.

At the top of the pyramid are what he called self-actualizing needs: the need to fulfil oneself, to become all that one is capable of becoming. Self-actualizing people are inclined to focus on problems outside of themselves, to have a clear sense of what is true and what is fake. They are spontaneous and creative, and are not all that concerned about social conventions. Many people never reach this stage of development. They will meet their other needs, but fail to get any further.

Maslow observed that self-actualizing people had more "peak experiences" than those people whose basic needs weren't being met.

Peak experiences are profound moments of love, understanding, happiness, or rapture; when a person feels more whole, alive, self-sufficient and yet a part of the world, more aware of truth, beauty, simplicity, harmony, goodness, and so on – some of the kinds of experiences I have labeled affairs of the soul. Maslow saw these peak mystical and transcendent experiences as the ones that inspired the founders of the great religions of the world including the nontheistic religions – Buddhism, Taoism, and Confucianism.

Maslow maintained that such ecstatic peak experiences are an almost universal phenomenon. He reached this conclusion after noticing that the more skilful he became in asking questions, the higher the percentage of his subjects reporting peak experiences. Like David Hay's research team, he suspected the problem wasn't that people weren't having these experiences; it was more that interviewees weren't being asked the right questions or given a sufficiently supportive atmosphere in which to talk about them. Eventually, Maslow concluded that everyone has probably had a peak experience. He used the label "non-peakers," not to describe those who hadn't had such experiences, but to describe those who were afraid of, had suppressed, or "forgotten" them.

"Non-peakers," he found, prided themselves on being completely rational and logical. These people tended to regard a peak or transcendent experience as a kind of temporary insanity. The complete loss of control terrified them, giving rise to their belief that they were being overwhelmed by "irrational" emotions which they vigorously fought off. Practical, means-oriented people also tended to see such experiences as producing nothing of value (since they earned no money), as untestable and as therefore being of no use and easily rejected.

Maslow observed that peak experiences often lead people to develop their own personal religion based on their personal discoveries and insights. From their point of view, God and meaning grow from private revelations, from which they develop their own myths and symbols. These may have the profoundest meaning to the individual, but hold little or no meaning for anyone else.[2]

The following story from my own files illustrates this.

The time was the early '80s, but I remember the sensation/ feeling/experience as vividly as if it were yesterday.

I had been seriously ill for some time and it was during one of my periodic stays in hospital – this time in a private single room. I was lying in bed and suddenly I felt a surge of warmth flow through my body. When I opened my eyes, I saw my physician – a deeply spiritual man – standing by the bed, head bowed as if in prayer. We chatted and he departed, but I could not get that "experience" out of my mind. For just for a couple of fleeting seconds, my entire being was flooded by some inexplicable "other" force or dimension.

I can't remember if I was hooked up to saline drip and a blood transfusion line, but my physician would not have adjusted the flow ration; the nurses performed those tasks. In any case, changes in the flow rates give me a shiver, not a warm surge.

How has it impacted my life? I don't know, except to say that during the different crises which have occurred since – not all medical – I've been able to work my way through most of them with a sense of inner calm and peace.

– Woman aged mid-60s

It's experiences such as this which build the privatized religious view Maslow referred to. This privatized religion also takes place within *institutional* religion. It may look as if a shared ritual is eliciting a collective religious response, but very often a radically different personal meaning or mythology is being taken from the same set of events, as this extended account shows.

—◉—

The experience itself was so dramatic – one of the healing points of my life, a real watershed. I had recently converted to Catholicism and was also participating in a training and development course exploring what shapes us as human beings. On this particular morning, I was at Mass. I went up to receive communion and as I stepped forward it was as if these waves of realization dashed themselves against me. These words formed inside me. Actually, "formed" is the wrong word. They were as clear as if I'd heard them spoken audibly, yet there was no sound. I sort of heard/knew them.

In separate waves I "heard," "You are good!" Crash. "You are loved!" Crash. "You are heard!" Thump. The image I had was that of these enormously deep, dark, completely unbridgeable crevasses being totally closed up and removed.

It wasn't as if I was a deeply troubled soul. I was happy, successful, and satisfied with life. But occasionally, in certain situations, I felt vulnerable, not good enough, and powerless. A part of me had a residual pocket of brokenness, emptiness, and despair, and it was this area that was utterly removed, gone in an instant. I was left feeling warm, loved, and accepted.

The words, "good, loved, and heard" may not mean much to someone else, but to me they were especially significant.

Good. I'd always been a good little girl, the model child, always happy, creative. Then one day, when I was about three years old, somebody told me the Devil would punish me if I was bad and so began a life avoiding this terrible fate. A life of being good,

nice, kind, thoughtful at all costs. I spent so much of my life trying to be good. Being good to people who were cruel to me, who
hurt me, who took liberties with me. The Pollyanna syndrome I
suppose. If they saw me as good, then they'd like me and maybe
give me an easier time. But it trapped me into some life courses
I didn't particularly like. My freedom to actually have a choice
was surrendered.

Loved. When I was nine years old, my parents, who seemed
perfectly happy to me (apart from a few food fights), divorced
suddenly! I'm sure I was the first child on the planet to have divorced parents in 1959. I know I was the first child in our school!
It's strange the way the human mind works because here was
the first *bad* thing that had ever happened in my life and it was
huge. Obviously (thought the three-year-old within) it's my fault.
If I'd been a really *good* girl, this wouldn't have happened. And
how could anyone really love me from now on?

Heard. My mum remarried – a man I wouldn't have chosen
as a stepfather. I tried to express this to my mum, but I never
quite found the right words to say to her. If only I'd been *heard!*
By now I was 14 and desperately trying to be good and loved, to
be all things to all people. As it turned out, my stepfather was
extremely violent when drunk and we spent four years swaying
between moderate happiness and absolute terror.

So the words "good, loved, and heard" brought me instant
floods of relief.

When you're bounced around as a kid, you tend to think
that somehow you caused it, that you're rejected and unloved
by your family not because they had a marriage break up but
because they didn't love you. Even though I was happily married and had kids of my own and my family really loved me I
had somehow always doubted it. Also, one of the reasons I had
stayed married was to show my parents that I wasn't like them;

I wasn't going to make my kids' lives miserable the way they had done to me!

These broken parts of myself had been well concealed by my highly successful career, wonderful marriage, and beautiful children. I'd managed, in spite of my early trauma, to have a wonderful life. However, that grace in Mass was confirmation that I have never been alone in anything. That my God has the power to totally heal and restore me, to complete me in spite of my brokenness.

From this one event things really changed for me. I realized I hadn't really chosen my husband for who he was; I had chosen marriage to prove others wrong. Released from this I saw things in a different light, re-evaluated my marriage, and made a conscious decision to choose him! It was so different from my original reasons for getting married that I wanted to get married again. He was a bit bemused by this, but I insisted. I earnestly wanted him to know that I had chosen him for who he was and this was my way of showing it. We arranged for a priest and one beautiful Saturday morning a few weeks later I stood once again in front of the altar and made my vows to my husband. It was a simple ceremony lasting about half an hour with only my children there as witnesses. Afterwards we went and had pizza.

Looking back on these events I realize how the simplest things can also be the most profound. In my experience, it seems to be the way God works.

– Actress aged 43

Privatized spiritual peak experiences like the one just described are seldom shared. Those who do so often live to deeply regret their disclosure. As Maslow observed, there is a tendency in many organized religions to develop "two extreme sides: the 'mystical' and individual on one hand, and the legalistic and organizational on the other."[3] The gulf that separates them is huge and is at the core of vicious and bloody splits in the ranks.

Maslow suggested that peakers naturally tend toward the mystical individual side, but that invariably it is the non-peakers, the practical organizational types, those who are deeply distrustful of such "out of control" experiences, who rise to the top of any complex bureaucracy, especially a religious one. Maslow asserted that this is one of the main reasons most religions eventually become hostile to the very experiences on which they were founded. Over time, the original vision of the prophet, seer, or mystic, is reduced to the dogmas and legalistic conventions of a religious hierarchy who safeguard and defend the "sacred."

It's like the story of the old cat that used to wander through the temple disrupting religious ceremonies. The priest eventually tired of this and arranged for the animal to be tied up during worship. Dutifully, just before each service, a lowly assistant was assigned the deed of restraining the cat. Eventually, the old cat passed away and was replaced by a younger cat. This one too, like its predecessor, was reverentially tied up before each service so it wouldn't annoy the worshippers. It became a ritual. Many generations passed and the original reason for the custom was lost. Hundreds of years later, learned scholars wrote long theological treatises on the sacred significance of a cat being tied up before worship services could proceed.

The harsh response some religious authorities direct towards those who trespass on "sacred" conventions and their suspicion regarding unorthodox spiritual experiences are two of the reasons people within religion are reluctant to share their soul affairs. But there is another even greater disincentive to share our soul affairs that occurs in both the religious and secular worlds:

our differing levels of spiritual maturity. Psychiatrist and author M. Scott Peck has condensed what he considers to be the stages of spiritual development into four broad levels.

- *Stage I, which I label Chaotic, Antisocial. In this most primitive stage people may appear either religious or secular, but either way, their belief system is profoundly superficial. It may be thought of as a stage of lawlessness.*
- *Stage II, which I label Formal, Institutional. This is a stage of the letter of the law in which religious fundamentalists (meaning most religious people) are to be found.*
- *Stage III, I label Skeptic, Individual. Here is where the majority of secularists are situated. People in this stage are usually scientific-minded, rational, moral, and humane. Their outlook is predominantly materialistic. They tend to be not only skeptical of the spiritual but uninterested in anything that cannot be proven.*
- *Stage IV, I have called Mystical, Communal. In this most mature stage of spiritual development, which may be thought of as one of the spirit of the law, women and men are rational but do not make a fetish of rationalism. They have begun to doubt their own doubts. They feel deeply connected to an unseen order of things, although they cannot fully define it. They are comfortable with the mystery of the sacred.*[4]

Peck cautioned that it pays not to jump to conclusions about who might be at what stage. For instance, someone who might outwardly appear to be a Stage IV mystic, such as a New Ager or scientist, might in truth be a fundamentalist. On the other hand, some evangelicals are Stage IV mystics.

The stages are basically developmental. You can't get to the next level without going through the lower one. This poses problems for some who take up a religious vocation at Stage II only to find a few years down the track that they're responsible for a parish or congregation and have to pay lip service to a God they no longer believe in. I have met many clergy like this. I have also come across profoundly spiritual Stage IV folk who have never been near a church.

Peck points out that the problem with the developmental process is that, apart from those at Stage IV, everyone is convinced that their stage is "it"; they are convinced that they have arrived and that those who are not with them are inferior. Stage II fundamentalists are convinced their particular revelation is not only the *right* or *only* answer, but that they have a God given authority to persuade others to their point of view. Stage III secularists, too, feel they've got the complete answer, but unless they are cornered by a fundamentalist they will be more covert about expressing their views. This leads to inevitable conflict.

However, for the average person who didn't ask for their soul affair, for whom it entered their consciousness quite uninvited, it can all be terribly confusing. How they react to their own soul affair will be determined by what stage of the spiritual maturation process they are currently in. The same is true for how others react to them. Were they to approach a priest who is a Stage III secularist their story would more than likely be dismissed. The same would apply if a soul affair were divulged to a non-peaker or a secular humanist. From Stage II fundamentalists, they would almost certainly receive a severe bruising since a spiritual experience via unorthodox channels (i.e. outside of the fundamentalist's religious context) is usually interpreted as illegitimate or evil.

Of course, the person who has taken the brave step of sharing their soul affair doesn't know why the person they're telling is reacting like this. They just get hurt. On the other hand, were they to describe their soul affair in traditional Western religious language they would run the risk of being branded a religious fanatic by the secularists, or embraced, for a while at least, by the fundamentalists. Both reactions would be anathema to those who have just had a mystical experience. The only receptive hearing they could hope for would be from someone who is at Stage IV. Unfortunately, there is no way of knowing who that might be until the subject is broached.

In the face of such religious and developmental complexity, it is no wonder that most of us who are spiritually unsophisticated often choose silence as the best option. In David Hay's survey the secretive nature of such affairs was found to be very common. People remained silent, Hay reported, because they didn't want to be thought of as mentally unstable, weird, or too "religious" and thereby lay themselves open to being mocked.

No, I've not told anyone. For the simple reason, there's such a lot of disbelievers about, and they'd ridicule you...

– A middle-aged factory worker[5]

I'd tell the wife. I don't tell me mates, otherwise they'd think I'd gone barmy.

– Male worker[6]

Never! [They'd] just laugh at me; well they'd probably listen but they wouldn't understand.

– Eighteen-year-old youth working in a shop[7]

A third of Hay's respondents admitted that they had either never told anyone else or had only dropped hints. When it came to experiences related to prayer, half had never told another living soul. With so very few trustworthy guides on such matters, we keep our privatized religious experiences and opinions to ourselves.

CHAPTER SIX

GUIDED BY AN UNSEEN HAND

The moment of truth, the sudden emergence of a new insight, is an act of intuition. Such intuitions give the appearance of miraculous flushes, or short-circuits of reasoning. In fact they may be likened to an immersed chain, of which only the beginning and the end are visible above the surface of consciousness. The diver vanishes at one end of the chain and comes up at the other end, guided by invisible links.

– Arthur Koestler[1]

Both Hay and Hardy received a large number of responses describing experiences of an unseen guiding hand and answers to prayer. The prayers tended to be those offered to God in the intimacy of solitude, with deep, heartfelt sincerity, rather than orthodox religious liturgies. The effect of such prayer was that people received answers to troubling personal problems or were instilled with a sense of encouragement and ability to do otherwise seemingly impossible tasks. Often what they "received" was able to be passed on to others. Such experiences dominated the accounts, as did times when people felt an unnamed presence beyond and outside of themselves. God acting benevolently for them, or through them for someone else. An invisible guiding hand.

Over 25 years ago, I had such an experience. It occurred when a friend and I were hitchhiking and weren't having much success.

We had been walking along a desolate road for a couple of hours and the occasional passing motorist seemed in no mood to pick up a couple of seedy looking long-haired youths. The fact that it had been raining steadily for the last hour made us an even less attractive prospect. Our jeans were wet, our shoes squelched, and our backpacks were soaked. We were traveling in high country and it was bitterly cold. Movement kept us warm and gave us something to do, so we plodded along in silence, pausing every once in a while to wave our thumbs hopefully at an approaching vehicle and then turn dejectedly back to the road ahead when they passed by.

We glumly considered giving up and turning back, but there seemed little point – we'd just be swapping one side of the road for the other and there was no reason to believe that folk going in the opposite direction would be any more inclined to pick us up.

Eventually, just on dark, someone took pity on us. As we eagerly hopped into the warmth of this spacious new car I could see the driver was having second thoughts. We dripped all over his new seat covers and our shoes left little pools of water on the expensive carpet. But to us it was luxury! I can even remember the make of car – a Rambler Rebel V8.

The driver obviously didn't like or appreciate us. In fact, he made it fairly obvious he would have preferred to have gone on past. He seemed surprised at himself for stopping, annoyed and slightly incredulous that he had allowed himself to lapse into a moment's pity. Yet despite his misgivings, something had possessed him to pick us up.

Sometime later, considerably rejuvenated, we were dropped off in the next town. I had a contact notebook with the address of a place we could stay, so we looked it up on the city map. Groan, it was three or four miles back the way we had just come! Way out on the town outskirts. But we had to go; there was nothing else we could do. Even if we could have afforded a motel it would have been unlikely we'd get accommodation, for in those days there was considerable prejudice against people who looked like us.

We started walking under the streetlights and as the miles rolled by the inner city turned to suburbs and then to very *posh* suburbs. Odd. This wasn't the sort of place we usually stayed – grubby student dives and run-down farmhouses were the norm. Strange. The suburb we were heading for also turned out to be very well-to-do. Eventually, we reached the street and the house. There must be some mistake; this was far too luxurious. Brick, two story, well-trimmed lawns and hedges. Damn, I must have misread the address.

We moved under a streetlight and I pulled out my notebook to recheck the address. But I couldn't find it. The address wasn't there! Neither the suburb, the street name, nor the street number. Gone. Completely disappeared. My friend checked too – nothing. *None* of the addresses we had for this city or any other address in my notebook in any way approximated where we had ended up. What was going on?

At that moment, some people emerged from the house and began getting into the cars parked outside. An elderly, well-dressed woman came to the end of the driveway to say goodbye. Seeing us standing there, she politely asked what we were doing. We told her what had happened. Did we know the people we were looking for? Well no, we were just hoping to find a floor to sleep on. (I thought she might be part of some church group and we'd be able to trade on a possible "do gooder" streak and ask her for a night's lodgings. But no, they had just finished a conservative political party meeting. Curses!)

But then, to my absolute astonishment, she said, "We've got a self-contained apartment downstairs. You can stay there if you like." A few minutes later, we were in complete luxury. Hot showers, fluffy towels, and clean sheets on real beds! We dared hardly speak in case it broke the spell or it turned out to be a dream. I felt cocooned, loved, cared for, and totally overwhelmed by what had occurred. It was as if some great unseen, unknown, benevolent process had brought us to sleep in my enemy's house (for in those anti-Vietnam War days, that's what I considered political conservatives to be) and had cared for me in spite of my outward appearance and internal prejudices.

Luck? Providence? God? Fate? Who knows? But I remember that moment today, decades later, as if it happened only yesterday. I remember the warm feeling that enveloped us that evening, and the sense of a benign presence, of a supervising or guiding hand, something much larger than any of the people who took part in this amazing sequence of events.

An experience of an unseen guiding hand like the one I've just described can be just as life changing and profound, if somewhat less intense, than the more mystical, almost orgasmic soul affairs. But just like transcendent moments they are unfathomable and defy logical explanations, which is one reason they are generally kept secret.

I put a religious name to my experience because I don't know how else it could have happened. Yet I am not a religious person, whatever that means. I do not belong to any denomination, or anything.

The event happened in 1985. I live in a country area and I often listen to the radio. One day I heard an interview of a lady from India. She was an English woman talking of her work in a Family Welfare Centre which she conducted in Indore.

While in Sydney, Australia, she had visited the zoo and was quite upset when she saw baby monkeys in humidicribs. The newborn Indian babies she rescued from rubbish bins, were nursed back to life in makeshift humidicribs – small cardboard boxes with cling wrap stretched over.

Without thought or hesitation, I telephoned the radio station and asked the receptionist to inform their guest that I would get her a humidicrib.

I am inclined to rush in and work things out afterwards. In this case, it was how to raise about $2,000 or more, where to buy a unit, and all the rest? I spent a terrible panicky day. That night, in bed, I said to "my" God, "How am I going to do this? You got me into it (blaming him), you had better give me an idea."

The next morning I had the answer. Simple and clear. Ring the nearest city General Hospital and ask if they have a spare humidicrib. When I rang and inquired, I was told they had a room full of superseded models, which were going to the dump. (What a wasteful nation we are!) It was decided at their next board meeting, held a couple of days later, that they would *give* me two.

As they are delicate, the units needed special packing care. I rang a removalist, who collected the machines and didn't charge for the specialized packing. The manager said, "Don't worry about the cost of the air freight, my friend is the local airline manager. I will fix it with him."

The units were sent to Sydney, where Air India took them on to India, and didn't charge for freight. The whole deal was finished in a fortnight. I didn't meet any of the persons who were part of the arrangement; it was all done by telephone and at no cost to me at all.

I received a letter of acknowledgment from the lady in India, who had returned by then. I have not kept in touch. I didn't know her or any of the people I contacted. They simply trusted my word and acted. There were no questions or difficulties.

Afterwards, I had a feeling that God had "used" me to fulfil a need. I thought that was pretty clever. I also thought it was a sign to prove to me that there *was* a God. It was a one-off experience, but that is all I should need if I was looking for proof. I wasn't aware of wanting to prove anything really. The event didn't change my life in that I didn't immediately rush to join a religious group. And I still have "my" God, in my way. Naturally, I thanked him.

I certainly floated about a bit afterwards. I suppose I had at the back of my mind that I might be saving a baby that might turn out to be another Gandhi or something. Maybe that was the reason it all went so smoothly, that there was a divine hand making sure it got done. I mean, I never moved from my home yet it all happened.

It was a unique experience, nothing like this has ever happened before or since and I've often wondered why me? It was one out of the box. I can't think of anything else like it. It's not as if I knew any of the people concerned, or had a network of contacts or that I was especially talented – I just felt used.

I would like to recapture the feeling I had. It is hard to explain, it was like being given positive directions knowing that everything I did was going to work out. I had no doubts, I wasn't surprised, I just knew. I suppose it would be too easy if life was like that all the time.

I can understand why people don't talk of these sort of experiences. I, at the time, did tell a few friends but I found as soon as I mentioned that it must have been God's plan, I was ridiculed. My experience was put down to the power of positive thinking and coincidence. Being in the right place at the right time. I don't agree. I know it was definitely different. It was a wonderful feeling, a complete take-over, yet I was still me!

– Female nurse aged 48

Lest the above account create a misleading impression, it is important to point out that not all the respondents to the Nottingham survey who experienced a guiding hand, nor those people I interviewed myself, identified "God" as the "source" of direction. Even more important, some of the experiences do not appear to have an overtly religious or spiritual aspect at all, although if given an opportunity, the respondent may provide one, as this last account illustrates.

I am a psychologist and family therapist working in private practice with children, adolescents, and adults with problems associated with intellectual disability, autism, and a range of other learning difficulties. I also work with their families and caregivers. My work and studies invite me to straddle between the worlds of hard science and the richness of human experience. Where my story fits in, I'm not sure. Maybe somewhere in-between, or maybe somewhere else altogether. My experience was clearly non-religious (for me), although deeply spiritual.

As the only child of migrant parents, I have known no extended family. As a youngster, however, family friends, themselves without children, assumed the role of doting grandparents and

sustained me through my developmental years. They were affec-
tionately known to me as "Auntie Estel" and "Uncle Ivan." Following Auntie Estel's death, Ivan turned their home, which they
had lovingly built with their own bare hands, into a virtual monu-
ment to Estel's life. From the day of her death, nothing was allowed to be touched or moved and he virtually closed the house
up to visitors. Ivan had always been a little eccentric, but now he
became virtually impossible for others to be with or respond to.
In the years prior to his own death, he became increasingly agitated and angry, as he struggled to make sense of the meaning of
his own life.

Ivan died at home nearly six years ago. In his will, he be-
queathed the vast majority of his considerable estate to the city
Art Gallery (he had been a prominent artist), with provision for
a small amount of money to be left to myself and a couple of
other old friends. While I had expected nothing from Ivan, I
found myself sad that he had thought the only thing of value to
give to others was his money. If I had allowed myself to want for
anything, I would have preferred a small memento by which to
remember Ivan and Estel. I had nothing of either of theirs. I
thought back and realized that Estel would have wanted me to
have something of hers, but Ivan had never thought to make
such an offering, as he was too consumed by his own grief.

Upon learning that all the contents of the house were to be
auctioned, I set my mind to the task of contemplating what
single thing from their home I might like, in order to capture
my memory of "Uncle Ivan and Auntie Estel." Surprisingly, I
found this choice rather easy – a little set of scraggly old red
painted wooden drawers. When I was a young child, these drawers had always resided alongside Auntie Estel's sewing machine.
She had used them to store all her sewing materials. As a toddler, I had spent many hours pulling and pushing these tiny

drawers open and closed. They were always full of sparkly buttons and beads, pretty fabrics, and endless rolls of wool and thread. Sometimes Estel would put a little treat (usually something she had made) in the drawers for me to find. It was a little girl's treasure trove. Some years later, the drawers were moved to Ivan's downstairs studio from where his prolific artworks emanated. The drawers then acquired a new life, as a home to Ivan's paints, brushes, pencils, special papers, and other art-related materials. Every time we visited, we would always go down to the studio to admire his work in progress. Over the years, the drawers became something of an artist's palette, with miscellaneous blotches and marks all over them. Ivan even used the underside of the drawers for sketching practice.

The auction was, as I expected, a very sad occasion. Remnants of a once rich life had been carelessly hurtled into cardboard boxes to be purchased for a song by money hungry secondhand dealers. Once-loved comfy old chairs sat dejected in the warehouse and personal possessions were strewn across tables for the world to see.

I went with my partner and mother who, while understanding my desire for a personal memento, found my choice a little odd. They were nevertheless supportive and both agreed that I should be able to purchase this apparently ugly set of drawers for around $20 – after all, they were not made out of good wood, they were in a poor state of repair, and they were covered in hideous red glossy paint. My partner agreed to bid on my behalf, as I was nervous. Bidding indeed started at a lowly $5 but continued between myself and one other person at an alarming rate. By the time it got to $50, my mother was muttering, "Don't be stupid. Let it go – it's not worth it."

As we got over $100, my partner became hesitant as I spurred him on. The usual background chatter of the auction room was reduced to stunned silence as this apparent piece of junk became a prize over which two people fought. I persisted and eventually procured the drawers for $320. My mother and partner slunk into the shadows with embarrassment as curious onlookers obviously wanted to know what kind of freak would exercise such incredibly poor judgment as to spend $320 on a piece of rubbish. I, on the other hand, was exhilarated and completely unconcerned about either the money or other people's opinions. I was just glad to have the drawers.

My partner and I loaded the drawers into the trailer and headed home. On the way home, my partner innocently asked if I would like to drop it off for an acid bath at the local antique dealer to remove the hideous paint. While I considered this possibility, I felt that I just wanted to get it home. As we were unloading the drawers, I noticed a tiny little wooden skewer poking out from the underside of the bottom drawer – it looked like the floor of the drawer had come loose at some stage and this was Ivan's patch up job. I didn't think anything of it. Upon placing the drawers down on their side and having another fiddle, a false bottom to the bottom drawer fell open, revealing its contents!

Ivan had obviously removed the items left sitting on Estel's bedside table following her death and placed them in this secret drawer. There were little scraps of paper with Estel's handwriting, a few pieces of inexpensive plastic jewelry which Estel had regularly worn, Estel's watch, a dress ring, and most precious of all, her wedding and engagement rings!

So what did all this mean to me? Well, I went into this whole exercise in pursuit of a way to capture my deep felt connection with Ivan and Estel. My attachment to this decrepit set of drawers was, of course, merely sentimental and symbolic. The auction itself felt like a test of my resolve to pursue that which was important to me. I felt that I came through with great strength.

The contents of the secret drawer were only a bonus, as I was entirely happy with the drawers alone. Nevertheless, to be so sentimentally rewarded for pursuit of this connection by the receipt of two rings which symbolized the connection Ivan and Estel shared with each other was enormously exciting. I also found myself having an overwhelming sense of being watched over and guarded (by Estel and Ivan) throughout this time. Without sounding cheeky, I know Estel would have wanted me to have her precious rings and would be delighted to know that they are so treasured. There was a strange circularity and sense of rightness about their safe passage into my care.

The message for me was "trust your intuition and remain steadfast in your resolve to pursue that which is important in life."

I now wear and love these rings. When I find myself feeling uncertain or out of sync with my own thinking, I catch a glimpse of Estel's rings and remind myself to trust my instincts and to pursue what I know to be right. I feel immensely privileged to have had such an experience and continue to be touched by it in my everyday life. That, to me, is what spirituality is about – being able to elicit meaning out the fabric of our lives in ways that enrich us and others.

I suppose that in writing this, I must also have a desire to tell my story. I probably haven't told it before (in writing), as the opportunity for the story to be appreciated for its spiritual significance has not presented itself to me.

– Female psychologist aged 35

CHAPTER SEVEN

DELVING DEEPER

Do our inner thoughts ever show outwardly? There may be a great fire in our soul, yet no one ever comes to warm himself at it, and the passersby see only a wisp of smoke coming through the chimney, and go along their way.

– Vincent Van Gogh[1]

Discovering Hay's research, Maslow's notion of peak experiences, and the concept of a spiritual maturing process, proved a huge relief. Until finding this documentation I had no idea that what I had experienced was so widespread and commonplace. As I delved deeper into David Hay's Nottingham survey, I discovered new information about the breadth and nature of the reports of God or a presence or power. It's worth briefly looking at more of his findings as they provide a framework for reading the anecdotal accounts.

Like my own, most of Hay's sample described the experience as totally involving, a vivid reality. The phrase "it was more real than me talking to you now," was a typical response. At the time of their experience many said their state of mind could be described as distressed or ill at ease (50%). Often the person was struggling with a serious issue such as losing their livelihood, the death of someone close to them or even their own death. But by the same token many others (34%) said there was nothing special going on. Only a few (5%) said they were praying or concentrating at the time. The majority (51%) of those who reported that their ecstatic experience lasted from a few seconds to ten minutes said it wasn't something they manufactured or had any control over, it just happened out of the blue, strengthening their belief that forces beyond their control were responsible.[2] Here from my own files is a very typical experience.

We had been married for six years and trying unsuccessfully to conceive a child for nearly three of those years. It doesn't seem like such a long time now, but back then it seemed like forever. Infertility is a great antidote for passion. Sex by the thermometer. Add to that anxiety, fear, embarrassment, guilt, the indignity of infertility tests and jealousy of friends' "successes." "We just need more practice," I'd joke. My laughter was hollow.

I guess I was praying throughout all this. I remember trying to bargain with God. If he'd just do this one thing for me, I'd trust him for the rest of my life. No response.

Things came to a head one cold May day. I was alone in my house. It was over 12 years ago, but I can picture myself vividly, sitting at my kitchen bench, my head in my hands. There was music playing, but I wasn't really listening to it. This infertility thing was getting me down. Although it was threatening to take over my life, I'd always been polite about it to God, like it didn't really matter. But it did. I was angry. Surely it wasn't such a big thing for him to do for me. I'd had enough. So I told him. I let him have it. All the anger, all the frustration, all the disappointment and hurt. Then I sat back, almost daring him to strike me dead for my impudence. It seemed a terrible thing to be angry with God.

But instead of being hit by a bolt of lightning, I had the unnerving sense that God was chuckling, perhaps even cheering, celebrating the fact that I had finally confided the truth about how I was feeling. I was astonished that he welcomed my anger. It seemed that at last we had reached a starting point. As I sat in the stillness and let the enormity of this settle, it was as if someone suddenly turned up the music and I heard the words, "When I stand in glory, I will see his face." I started to weep. The weeping gave way to heart-rending sobs. For the first time in my life, I knew in the depths of my being that it was true and in an instant nothing else mattered. My agenda was insignificant. It was as if I was suddenly standing outside myself, looking over the shoulder of someone filming my life. In an instant, the film abruptly zoomed out to a scene like something out of a James Herriot novel – a broad, expansive, peaceful place of gentle green hills – a place where you want to draw deep breaths and let the air fill your lungs.

The bit that had been my life was a tiny speck, off to the left of the center of the picture. All of the struggling and stuff I'd been through gained a new perspective. Although I was so small, I felt affirmed. I had a place in all this. There was nothing for me to decide or to evaluate. This was just the way it was.

In a matter of seconds, or maybe not even that long, everything had changed. I had thrown a temper tantrum like a child. I had vented my anger and I'd been broken, but that was okay. There was no sense of recrimination. But my thinking had changed. Everything was fine. Everything was in place. I knew I was perfectly safe.

I knew it was God because all these events, these feelings, came from nowhere, they weren't from me. I hadn't created or prompted any of this. It was totally unexpected. I was penetrated by something enormous and powerful. I was overwhelmed by the potency of it. It's difficult to describe, but I knew it was real. My emotions changed so powerfully and dramatically in a matter of seconds, even less, and nothing else had happened except this stuff in my head. And it was so positive, not warm and fuzzy, but strong and positive.

I had known and sincerely loved God for as long as I could remember, my life revolved around the church, but I'd never known anything like this. It was so direct, clear, immediate, unexpected. I wasn't sitting there trying to analyze "What does this mean?" or "Is this for me?" I just knew. I knew all I needed to know, and I was content not to be concerned with anything else. I felt safe, cared for, part of the whole.

I've always accepted the traditional church concept of God and the possibility of one day being with him in heaven, but all that had been head knowledge – in this moment it became real. It was as if someone famous I had read about and admired all my life suddenly turned up on my front doorstep. I would be astonished that they knew me, let alone taken the time to visit me. But this was so much more, this was God!

Looking back now, I can't list for you the ways all of this changed my life. It makes me sad in a way, because it seems I betrayed an amazing gift. But then again, I didn't feel anything was expected of me in return. After all, it was a gift. It's ironic that I had spent over 20 years trying to please God, and now, when I threw a tantrum, he came through in a way he never had before. He became real.

Several months later I became pregnant, so that was a significant change! However, I wouldn't say there was necessarily a direct connection between the two events. In the years since, I have never deliberately thrown a tantrum again to get my own way with God, so it wasn't as if I seized upon a formula to manipulate him. It was much, much bigger than that. I had been overwhelmed with the issue of my infertility but in a matter of seconds I was abruptly and astonishingly overwhelmed by infinitely larger events. So even though this pregnancy ended in miscarriage, I still felt I could trust him, no matter what happened. Of course I was upset, but my world didn't fall apart. Something must have changed in the way I had been freed from worry and fear, and been given an ability to trust in a power infinitely larger than me – what I call God. I subsequently had two great kids.

I don't recall telling anyone about this at the time, but later on I told a few people the vaguest outline, only a couple of sentences. I described it as the first time I knew God was real.

– Female teacher aged 41

Like this woman, most of Hay's respondents in the extended follow up interviews were comfortable asserting that what they had experienced was "God," based on their Western concept of the divine.

It makes you feel there is a power you can call God or the Life Force.[3]

When you're brought up that way, you just see things that way. (p. 155)

– Working class woman aged 33

Many became irritated when asked if they saw their experience as "religious," thinking it a stupid question – what else could it be? Some were willing to concede that in another culture they might well give it a different name, but they weren't particularly perturbed by such a suggestion.

Something woke me up. There was something or somebody by my bed; I wasn't frightened. Within ten minutes the torment I'd felt, for some strange reason left me. I think I had more peace then than I'd had for a very long time…I have enough knowledge to know that there's somebody there, to know that I need never be so alone again…he decided I needed help.

When asked who "he" was, the respondent said, "Jesus, I suppose." (p.139)

Ironically, these "religious experiences" rarely occurred in religious places such as a church or within a church service. The majority occurred when the respondents were either completely alone or alone in a non-religious public setting (70%).[4]

I'd been walking in the woods alone and it was on coming out of the woods and looking towards the fields over a gate that I had a sort of visual image of everything being brighter and larger than life and at the same time I had this feeling of understanding and being a part of it…I didn't think I would tell you about it. (p. 153)

Asked how they felt after the experience, over two-thirds described themselves as feeling at peace, restored, happy, elated, uplifted, awestruck, exhausted, or numb. For some it confirmed their beliefs. For others it made them more optimistic, gave them new insights into life or encouraged moral behavior.[5]

I feel God's always with me; it's confirmed and strengthened the things I've been brought up to know; given me the will-power to go on.

— Young married woman (p. 158)

It's made me happier for most of the time. Although I get scep-tical feelings now and again, they don't matter because now I know.

— Young man whose experience gave him relief from personal anguish (p. 158)

Well I've certainly been a lot happier. I've been able to mix with people more. More at ease with life.

—Factory charge hand (p. 158)

It completely changed my viewpoint, my philosophy of liv-ing. Instead of thinking that everything could be decided on the basis of reason, I realised that the deeper things were intuitive...

— 24-year-old graduate (p. 159)

I behave better; it touches the conscience.

— Retired factory packer (p. 159)

Almost three-quarters of Hay's respondents said that the longer term outcome of their experiences was that it changed their atti-tude toward life to some extent. Such a changed outlook is one of the traditional criteria religious experts use to determine whether or not a religious experience is authentic. Judged on this criteria alone it appears the overwhelming majority of respondents are genuine.

A handful of respondents had experienced negative or evil powers. Although television shows and horror films might lead us to believe such events occur frequently, both Hay's study and Hardy's letters contain only a very small proportion of such accounts.

I was out one night in Sussex…and when I came to a ruined building, I felt the presence of something evil, which made me feel extremely uncomfortable and frightened…on no other occasion in my life have I had such an overpowering feeling of the presence of evil… (p. 148)

Most of Hay's responses seemed to fall broadly into the same categories as the 3,000 letters Hardy had collected, the only exception to this being a substantial number of accounts featuring the presence of the dead. The following experience occurred to a man after a marriage breakup.

I felt a presence somehow, in my bedroom, and I thought it was my old grandmother who'd been dead for some years. I could have sworn I saw her there and I spoke to her in Welsh. She said, "You are in trouble my son and I may be able to help you."…I believe there's a God and the power of God can overcome anything. My grandmother appeared through the power of God. (p. 144)

This next incident occurred when the respondent was holidaying in Ireland.

When I got to the boat I felt the presence of my mother. It gave me a saintly feeling, it's hard to explain...to me it was very, very real...almost as if she were at my shoulder all the time, as if I was walking on air, a wonderful experience.

When asked what it meant to her, she replied, "You seem to come nearer the Lord don't you, really? To me it seemed like a miracle; actually you can't put it into words really, very deep rooted peace of mind...When there's arguments about religion, when they scoff, that's when I'd like to tell them, but then they'd think there's something wrong with you." (pp. 144–145)

Answered prayer and experiencing the presence of God was a big category in both Hardy's letters and Hay's surveys.

I've been interested in God and what it meant since my teens, and during the study of Victorian poetry, particularly Tennyson and Browning and their searchings for God, I thought about their problems which seemed relevant to me. I began praying, not really sure that there was a God. At one particular time there was (after a great deal of thought) – a great relaxation came upon my mind and everything fitted together. It only lasted for a moment, perhaps four to five seconds...I really felt God was communicating with me. (p. 139)

The following account is from a young history candidate.

When I was thirteen, and my father became ill, I began to feel as though I needed something else in life, and seemed to find the answer in prayer...for about two years this whole experience seemed very real to me, and my belief in this "some-thing," which I called God at the time, was very strong. It was a very personal feeling, just between me and "God," and I never made any attempt to tell others of my beliefs. But I think it did give me comfort, even if what I was ultimately asking for was not granted. I think it probably meant more to me then than it does now, my memory being coloured by my present attitudes (of agnosticism). (pp. 140–141)

The mention of agnosticism here raises one of the most intriguing aspects of the British national opinion poll survey. When asked to identify their religious denomination nearly a quarter (23–24%) of those who'd had an experience of a presence or power (whether they called it God or not) identified themselves as being either "agnostic," "atheist," or "don't knows."[6]

I'd say it was an intoxication with the sights, sounds and forces of nature. A feeling of power coming through my body from internal and external sources…I can't distinguish what is divine and what is temporal. It's nothing to do with the Christian God. (p. 143)

Hay surmised that in many cases perhaps "agnostic" and "atheist" were simply labels used by respondents to show their rejection of traditional Christian views rather than a carefully thought out philosophy.

However, at the other end of the religious spectrum, among those who attended church either regularly or occasionally, almost half (44%) said they had never been influenced by a presence or power whether they called it God or not! This led the researchers to conclude that there is "no reason to suppose that people who are in touch with the experiential dimension of religion will necessarily be churchgoers."[7]

This interesting phenomena also showed up in a poll taken in the United States in 1998. A nationwide survey conducted by the Barna Christian Research Group revealed that one-third of the 75 million adults who regularly attend American Christian church services say that they have never experienced God's presence at any time during their life.[8] It appears that experiential spirituality is widespread and exists quite independent of the religious institutions.

Premonitions also featured in the reports, but religious interpretations of such events were unusual.

Surprisingly, the Nottingham survey and the letters received by the Religious Experience Unit uncovered very few sudden and dramatic "Road to Damascus" or "gutter to glory" religious conversions. This is indeed unusual given their prominence in historical records of religious experience and their emphasis in evangelical Christian groups.

However, the overall demographics of those reporting religious experiences were similar to the demographics of church attenders, especially the higher numbers of women. Consistently in all the research, women were more likely to report an experience, supporting a commonly held view that women are more comfortable with religion, prayer, otherness, and the more intuitive aspects of life.

More recent polling in the UK and in other countries shows that the numerically smaller, more conservative fundamentalist denominations generally have much higher reporting rates (68%[9]–81%[10]) than the mainstream Catholic, Anglican, and Protestant denominations. Perhaps this is due to the affirmation charismatic and pentecostal denominations give to public testimonies of religious experience.

As the results were analyzed, Hay was at first puzzled to discover that better off, more educated respondents were more likely to report an experience. "The reason for my initial surprise was that when social scientists think of 'experiential' religion they tend to have in mind a variety of pentecostal and messianic sects, of a type which are usually found among people who have been socially deprived. As well as that, working-class people seem to be more superstitious than others. They are more likely to have a lucky mascot, have a lucky number, to have visited a fortune teller, to read their horoscope regularly, and to believe in ghosts. Sometimes people are inclined to lump religious experience and superstition together, but on this evidence it looks as if they should be treated separately."[11]

The link between higher education, social class, and religious experience was later found to hold true in American studies. Hay surmised this was because the better educated and affluent were more likely to have had contact with religious organizations through their schooling and families, so "coming from a background that has words and traditions that respect this area of human experience perhaps allows people to be open to it."[12]

Generally, those who'd been exposed to church would use the word "God," those with little or no contact with institutionalized religion tended to use the words "a higher power."

Hay also commented that using the label "religious experience" for what his respondents were describing was somewhat dissatisfying. Because much of what was reported falls well outside religious orthodoxy, it would be treated extremely cautiously by institutionalized religion. On the other hand, agnostics and atheists would also be extremely uncomfortable with the term "religious experience." "It would be more correct to say that it is a type of experience which is commonly given a religious interpretation."[13]

There was a comparatively small number (15%) of respondents who said they had more of a continuous awareness lasting months or even years, one which they seemed to be able to access at will. These folk reported more tranquil, much less ecstatic moods than those whose experiences were unpredictable.[14] Maslow, too, makes mention of what he termed the "plateau experience." Rather than a climactic, awesome and miraculous feeling, a plateau experience is characterized by a serene calm. There are countless books, courses, and studies that document how to achieve such states through meditation or prayer. Indeed this is the route along which traditional religion will steer individuals interested in connecting with God. My interest, however, is in the much more common and widespread experience of a presence or power, or God, coming uninvited to the uninitiated.

Since the first British opinion poll was done, similar surveys have been conducted throughout the English speaking world, with similar results. It appears that a large proportion of the Western population has had firsthand experience of God or a presence or power. Similarly worded questions in surveys returned a 43% positive response in the United States (1985)[15], 44% in Australia (1983)[16], and 44% in Canada (1990)[17]. Although the experiences are widespread and common, they usually occur only once or twice in a lifetime. This was perhaps one of the reasons why older people tended to have higher reporting rates – they had had more years in which to experience their "moment."

Hardy and Hay's research is fascinating not only because it amply demonstrates the nature, form, and frequency of experiences of a presence or power (God), but also because to the best of my knowledge it is the only objective qualitative study that so seriously and extensively documents the topic.

I knew without a doubt that my own passionate affairs of the soul were real and profound, but thanks to my cultural conditioning I was convinced that I must be some sort of fruitcake to have had them. I was completely unaware that what I had experienced was normal, that like romantic love, soul affairs are a common experience, a typical part of being human. Herein might lie much of the reason our culture continues to believe in such concepts as God and the soul, despite the overwhelmingly logical and convincing arguments against them. Far from God or a "higher power" being dead, to most Westerners he/she/it is alive and well and living in their hearts, just seldom on their lips.

As I became increasingly excited about all this, I began to accumulate a collection of soul affairs told to me by friends, acquaintances, and colleagues. Often when I mentioned the subject matter of this book people had a story to tell. Because I was already known and trusted they knew their account wouldn't be cross examined, scrutinized, or ridiculed, that it would instead be honored and accepted. Under these circumstances, I was privileged to hear many confidences. Some stories are from people I have worked alongside for years never knowing that they, like me, had had such dramatic affairs of the soul.

Consistent with the research, the majority of people relating these experiences are non-superstitious, educated, fully functioning, absolutely sane citizens who, just like me, raise families, work, recreate, and enjoy life. They are definitely not abnormal, mentally unhinged or easily given to flights of fancy. It's more than likely that as you read the accounts in the next chapter they will trigger memories and experiences of your own.

CHAPTER EIGHT

UNSEEN AND UNTOLD

Whenever we encounter the Infinite in man, however imperfectly understood, we treat it with respect. Whether in the synagogue, the mosque, the pagoda, or the wigwam, there is a hideous aspect which we execrate and a sublime aspect which we venerate.

– Victor Hugo[1]

Back in 1971, I attended an accounting conference, which was held by the firm I worked for. It was all quite grand – overnight accommodation provided at a large hotel.

The day before the conference I was told I had been chosen as one of the group leaders and hence as spokesman for my group. The firm was large and there would be quite a number in attendance. Not being a leader, I felt worried and ill at ease. I cannot remember how I spent the rest of the day.

That night while in bed a small glimmer of light occurred in my mind and it gradually expanded until it seemed that there was only this wonderful golden yellow comforting light and my awareness of it and all I wanted to do was to remain in this light forever. It was all that mattered…being bathed in that wonderful light.

I can remember that event, and always will, as an outstanding experience in my life.

They say the brain produces substances under stress. I prefer to accept it as a comforting gift in a time of need. I was very alone at that time with family troubles.

Another experience occurred maybe a year later. Things hadn't improved on the family front. I was alone in our apartment; my wife and children were visiting her parents.

I had been washing the walls in this big old apartment in anticipation of their return. But somehow I knew it was the end; the family was finished; they were never coming back.

I broke down under the loneliness and the loss, and lay down on the frayed and shabby carpet. A while later I got up and took myself outside, it being a sunny Sunday afternoon.

There was hardly any traffic and everything was quiet. I walked along this street and looked up and was surprised to see everything was shimmering, as though everything belonged to each other, nothing was separated and on its own. The concrete footpath and telephone poles belonged to the clouds and the trees and the houses and fences, and everything was in harmony with everything else and I remember myself thinking that I wished I was able to see like that always. I wanted to have that way of seeing the harmony of everything as a permanent state of mind. I walked along the street willing myself to hold on to this understanding or new awareness and came to this little shop window. In a vase was an amazing vibrancy of color from the flowers.

This experience only lasted about five minutes and I have had nothing similar to either of them since.

The experiences didn't make me a better person or change my life. All I know is that there are other dimensions to this world that are not so obvious and you only get a glimpse of such things if you are exceptional, maybe.

– Man aged 68

As with the act of sexual union, people experiencing overwhelming mystical moments – such as the one above where the respondent was bathed in wonderful light – temporarily lose their physical and psychological boundaries. They become transcendent. These are extraordinarily powerful moments. Often when the stories were shared tears would flow as something resonated deep inside both teller and listener. This was something the Nottingham researchers had noted and I too had personally experienced. When talking about my own soul affairs, suddenly and unexpectedly I would be overcome with tears. They were not tears of joy or sadness – just something inexpressible triggered deep within.

The following story comes from a man now in his 70s. The experience he relates occurred in the early 1950s.

At the time this happened I was in terrible trouble, terrible personal turmoil. He, a spiritual personage, appeared and told me he was going to take me to see somebody in the garden of Gethsemane.

I expected to see this beautiful garden – with shrubs, flowers, trees, and birds – a beautiful garden. But instead of that there was an old piece of iron railing, a gnarled old tree which looked like nothing on earth. It looked as if all the animals of the earth had been eating off the ground and there was hardly a blade of grass left on it. This wonderful figure was standing in the corner and he said, "Come to me my son, walk with me in the garden," and he took me for this wonderful walk in the garden of Gethsemane…

At this point in the conversation, the elderly gentleman broke off as great sobs welled up in him. The almost half century of time between that moment and now was but an instant. His experience had lost none of its impact. It still touched him to the core. He apologized for weeping so openly, but explained there was little he could do about it. Retelling the experience moved him so. It always had. As he revisited the affair, his emotions spoke eloquently of the poignancy of his story. It was as if he was sharing a piece of his soul.

After regaining his composure he continued and tried to encapsulate what he had felt at that time.

I was absolutely thunderstruck. Words just can't describe what it was like. Although we walked we didn't seem to be moving. He talked to me all the time we were "walking" but I can't remember a word that he said, anything at all. It was wonderful.

In that moment if I'd had nine lives it was as if I'd lived them all at once.

It was a tangible intangible. It was an appreciation of creation. The power that surpasses all things – wonderful – it's like a symphony starting, an iridescent cascade of sound and sight.

There was nothing religious in this whatsoever, it's only spiritual. I've never felt in the remotest bit religious – spiritual yes, religious no.

Such stories come not from folk who seek the limelight, or who are exhibitionist by nature. On the contrary, most were extremely coy in divulging details and have done so simply to help flesh out the nature of such affairs. Often the experience is so intense we're shocked by its overwhelming profundity, the like of which we've never previously known.

—◉—

I was driving through the mountains on a beautiful summer day. I was relaxed, unwound, open, stress free. I was alone, aware of superb scenery, but had to keep my eyes on the road. The road, in one section, was dirt and I found that part of the drive quite nerve-racking. Eventually, I reached a lookout point and stopped to take a breather. When I walked onto the viewing platform, I gasped, not just at the beauty of the vast mountainous landscape before me, but I was gripped by a sort of awe and fear at the scene and at the creator of this environment. I suppose I felt the power of the creative force behind that environment. I felt so small, and the power of the creator was so palpable. I felt quite shaken by all this. However, at the same time, I felt connected to creation and this fearful creator of it. I might be small, but I was a tiny cog, a part of the hugeness. I had a place in it, a purpose. So I felt drawn in and at the same time overwhelmed. I was meant to be there and to be a part of the world.

It was my first experience of being a bit scared of God. I was uncomfortable with it at first – it was a connection with creation, a confronting experience, and it shattered my previous "comfortable" faith.

I used to think it personal. This was much bigger than I anticipated. It was quite unfathomable, a multifaceted God. I mean, they speak about the Holy Trinity, but why stop at three?

I came away with fear and a sense of purpose – there was a sense of me being meant to be there.

– Female teacher aged 35

A number of people related experiences where someone they'd been close to had died and had made their presence felt afterwards.

I first met Neil when I was training for triathlons. He was my coach. We'd meet and cycle many kilometers together. Even though there was at least a 35-year age gap, somehow we just clicked. We'd talk about anything and everything for hours. He always knew when I was down and would say, "What's up, girl?" All those who knew us spoke of the special rapport we seemed to have.

Two years ago, I had a baby and it wasn't possible for me to meet and cycle with him, but I still made a point of chatting with him whenever I could, usually on the weekends.

Neil developed lung cancer and for 12 months he was in a succession of hospitals and hospices. I used to visit him when I could.

One evening, about two weeks after I had last seen Neil, I was woken up just before midnight by the sound of my toddler's toy playing a song. The house was quiet, the baby was asleep and I was puzzled as to what had made this toy spontaneously start playing as it was on its own on a table in the lounge room. I picked it up and it began playing another song. As I looked up, I could feel this presence. As if someone else was in the room with me. At first I wanted to check to see if the baby was all right, but then I thought I didn't have to because it felt like a good presence, a good spirit. It was a warm feeling.

The next day my mother told me that Neil had died the previous day.

I think that the presence I felt that night in the room was Neil coming to say goodbye. To sort of acknowledge me before he went to his place of peace. I certainly felt peaceful about it. I wasn't scared or apprehensive or anything like that.

In some way I wasn't surprised about these events. I somehow "knew." It wasn't scary or freaky, actually quite the opposite – I just felt totally at peace that things were right between Neil and I and that he was in a good place.

I don't know whether it's got anything to do with God. I believe we go to a better place, a place of peace, when we die – heaven or whatever, and that's where Neil was headed. I think he just wanted to acknowledge me and the end of "us," to say goodbye that one last time.

– Female TV producer aged 34

The number of stories of contact with the deceased was the only major difference between Hardy and Hay's research. Hardy received relatively few accounts of contact with the dead, whereas for Hay, as indeed for me, it was reported much more frequently. From the accounts I considered, this next person also suspected that their experience was related to someone who had recently died.

I am a telephone counselor for under 19-year-olds who are in crisis. A kids' help line. I absolutely love my job as it presents me with new challenges each day and I learn so much. I have no opinion on the events I experienced. Rather, I put myself in the position of a skeptical, detached observer and try to keep a realistic perspective. That's the challenge.

This experience occurred in late 1992. A female teen (16) I had been counseling had suicided, tragically. She'd told a friend that if anything did happen to her the friend was to contact me. Through our telephone counseling sessions, we'd got close and I suspect I was one of the few people she'd ever opened up to as she was generally distrustful of people. I sensed our relationship might have been unique for her, that I might have been the only person she talked to about the things going on her life.

This client had been struggling to gain control of herself for some time and when I gained news of [the suicide] I was very shocked and saddened. That night after work, I went to bed. It was around 10 p.m. As I lay there in bed, my mind went over the sessions I'd had with this client. I became quite emotional, weeping a bit, just grieving in a way for her. I decided to try to go to sleep.

About half an hour later as I was drifting toward sleep, I was brought back to full consciousness and alertness by an unfamiliar sensation. With my eyes still shut I felt a warm tingling feeling pass down from the tip of my head through to about my shoulders. A couple of seconds later, with my eyes still closed I began to "see" an image of a girl's face. Still with eyes shut, I noted her face coming, sort of floating right up close. Behind the transparent face was a bluish-white colored ball of light with hundreds of little needles of light radiating from it. The image of the girl was a very melancholy one, but she seemed to be giving out a reassuring feeling. I felt quite touched by this image reaching out to me. After about 10 to 20 seconds, the image began to fade and move out of my view. It was not unpleasant at all, but I can't to this day quite understand what happened that night.

At the time I did not stop to analyze what was happening as it was a very relaxing and reassuring and friendly experience. I just let it happen. It seemed natural and I wasn't in the least bit shocked or discomforted. Rather, I let the experience take its course.

It's hard to describe really – it was hard to say I was "seeing something" because my eyes were shut, but somehow through my mind visual images were being created. It wasn't just visual either, it was a totality of feeling, it all had a melancholy sadness about it, but somehow reassuring at the time, like she was on a continuation or a natural sequence of going to sleep from a state of wakefulness. It was definitely something I had no forewarning of or anything I in any way initiated.

I remember thinking to myself, "Gee, what's happening?" then afterwards, "What was that!" Maybe it was the girl. I was certainly feeling intense emotions about her, I hadn't contrived it in any way.

I'm not too shocked or surprised by things that come out of the blue. I suppose I have an increased openness to the unexpected. I'm more interested in our earthly existence and questioning ourselves. I've certainly got every reason to question the accepted science of who we are and what we are. I think there may be other explanations that we're not aware of.

I'm open-minded about religion. Certain tenets of Christianity and other faiths appeal to me but I believe in what I perceive. I suppose I'd have a strong faith in my own perception.

– Male youth counselor aged 29

Here from another young person is an experience of a recently deceased person making their presence felt.

It was a year and a half since my brother had died and I was having a dream one night. I dreamt I was with my friends in a hallway and one of my friends said, "Isn't that your brother at the end of the hall?"

He was just sitting on a seat next to the door and I walked down to him asking, "Is that you? Is that you?"

He was saying "yes" and I reached out to touch him. I expected him not to be there as I was dreaming, but I physically touched him and then I threw my arms around him and was crying and saying, "I'm so glad you're back."

I don't even remember waking up, but the next minute my outstretched arms caught the mirror that usually sits on the windowsill next to my bed. The cat had knocked it down while I was dreaming, and had I not been sitting up with my arms outstretched to hug my brother it would've landed on my face. I'd hate to think what damage it might have done as it was a big heavy mirror, about a meter round with a large beveled wooden frame.

After the dream, I put the mirror back up on the windowsill. I wasn't freaked out or afraid or anything. I just had this incredible sense of peace about me. I spoke out loud to my brother. "Wow, thank you." I truly believe he saved me from being hurt.

I don't have any reason or logical explanation for this dream and for me catching the mirror, but I know it happened and it's as real as me sitting here talking to you now.

– Waitress aged 21

This same woman went on to describe the unusual events that occurred around the time of her brother's death.

I was in a van with a whole lot of friends traveling to another city. It was about an hour or two's journey and we were all laughing and singing. Everybody was having a great time. We were playing some cassettes on the car stereo and singing along at the tops of our voices when all of a sudden the words we were singing just hit me. It was about everybody being hurt sometime and as the song went on I was suddenly overcome by this feeling of deep sadness – even a hurt. There was no reason for it. I was so happy one minute and then the next I was overwhelmed by these incredibly intense feelings. I didn't know what to make of it. It lasted about 10 or 15 minutes and I sort of withdrew from everyone else, even though I could still hear what was going on. Someone eventually asked me if I was okay – I said I was just thinking. This uneasy feeling stayed at the back of my mind for the rest of the day. I couldn't stop thinking about it.

When we drove home that afternoon we went back to the office and the secretary said somebody's mum had been desperately trying to get hold of one of us, but she couldn't remember who. I said, "It can't be my mum because she's at work," but even as I said it deep in my heart I knew it was her.

Usually, every afternoon after work I'd go around to Mum and Dad's work (they have a small business) but for some reason I didn't that day. I skylarked around with my mates. I don't know why, but I kept finding excuses not to go to their work or home, as if I was avoiding something, but I didn't know what.

We ended up at a friend's place later on that day making some stupid videos, just mucking around with the camera. At one point we had to go to another house to get a video player and on the way back another feeling, this time of absolute dread, came over me, so much so that I felt physically sick. I just pulled on the handbrake and ran into the park and vomited on the grass. My friends thought it was a great laugh and videoed the whole thing!

I felt really weird. It wasn't a tummy bug or something. Usually when I vomit I feel nauseous for a while beforehand, but this was instant, brought on by the feeling of dread. I recovered pretty quickly and we went on to another park.

We were just sitting down and the mother of one of the guys in our group drove into view. I somehow knew she hadn't come for him; she'd come for me. It was horrible the way she jumped out of the car and ran over the footbridge towards me. It was f— ing horrible. I never want to feel that way again. She was really upset and agitated and yelled, "You've got to come with me," and dragged me by the hand to the car. All the time I was trying to pull away from her because she wouldn't tell me what was wrong. I was screaming at her by this stage and she was getting madder at me and all the while this is going on there was almost like a voice inside of my head telling me my life was never going to be the same again. I knew someone was seriously hurt, maybe Mum or Dad or my brother.

She drove me to my parents' factory and as we pulled up outside I could see my brother's car was there and I thought at least he was okay – it must be Mum or Dad.

I ran in and saw Mum at her desk and Dad standing beside it. I instantly knew it was my brother. I knew he wasn't badly hurt, or anything. I just knew he was dead. It was the worst feeling in the world. I later learned he'd died of a brain hemorrhage at the gym around the time I experienced that first feeling of deep sadness in the van. Suddenly everything fell into place and the day made awful sense. He was only 21.

It definitely wasn't a coincidence. I mean how do you explain something like that? It's not the sort of thing you make up or muck around with. I'm talking about my only brother here. There was only me and him; we were the only kids in our family. I trust my experience of it. I know what happened and I know how it felt. What others make of it doesn't matter. Besides, I'm still on video vomiting!

The following accounts show that often in these experiences our actual physical senses, along with our intuition become involved.

Once I was taken to my father's birthplace by my brother. My mother was also there. Before he died it had been his dream to take us all back one day to his home. We were sitting in my elderly aunt's kitchen having afternoon tea, when I was aware with all my being of a perfume so strong and fragrant it made me gasp. I said to my mother, "Can you smell a beautiful perfume?" She could not and neither could my brother or aunt. I *know* my father was there.

– Woman aged 64

This next account also involves a daughter and her father.

I was brought up in a rural area. I'm tertiary educated, Catholic, very gregarious, creative, and quite an extrovert. I consider myself open and receptive and have a healthy skepticism – not easily influenced by fads and trends – I have to experience things for myself.

Before this experience, my father, who was in his 60s, telephoned to tell me he'd had some tests and they'd discovered tumors in his lungs. That night I was awoken around 2:00 a.m. by the sound of my heart breaking. I know that sounds really odd, but that's what it was. I heard it crack and felt my chest sort of splitting. It was massive, sudden, and explosive.

The next morning I did all my usual early morning things and got into the car to drive to work. I was sitting at a set of traffic lights when I became aware of/felt this pressure on the side of my face. I distinctly remember that the pressure was that of a cheek lightly pressed against mine, sort of cuddling me. The feeling I was filled with at this time was one of love and support – it felt fine. I then felt a hand holding my hand and "felt" it had no middle finger. I knew this because there was no pressure in this area. And then it dawned on me. I realized it was my dad's hand; he'd lost his middle finger in a building site accident when I was a little girl.

I continued on to my first appointment which was a short one and I returned home after an hour to be met by my husband words, "Your dad's gone." Apparently he'd died from a massive heart attack during the night. I wasn't at all surprised. In fact, I half expected it after the events of the previous few hours.

I don't know whether I'd call it an act of "God," but it was definitely from the good side of the spiritual realms. Maybe God works through those that are close to us; perhaps it's similar to the way the saints do it. I really don't know and it doesn't concern me all that much. I just accept that I've been given a great grace.

But there was more to come. An interesting thing happened a few years later when I picked up my then six-year-old son from school. As he hopped into the car he quite nonchalantly said, "I saw Puppa today and he gave me a message to tell you." (Puppa was his name for his granddad.)

"Puppa?"

"Yes. He told me to tell you that he's very proud of you."

As soon as he finished telling me this, he skipped on to telling me the next topic of his day, as if seeing and talking to Puppa was a normal part of his routine! Kids are just so accepting of what we adults would probably get quite alarmed over. He saw absolutely nothing unusual or abnormal in being visited by his dead grandfather.

But my small son's words were very significant. I'd been deeply troubled by the events that transpired the last time I'd seen Dad alive. He lived in a country town a long way from the city I was currently living in and I didn't get many opportunities to see him. A few weeks before he died we visited him for the weekend. As I prepared to leave late on Sunday afternoon, he asked me, with tears in his eyes, to stay another day. "Do you have to go?"

As much as I wanted to stay, I couldn't as I had arranged to take the family to my in-laws who always made sure our visits to them were as long as the visits to my family – if not we'd never hear the end of it! I had all these "shoulds" in my head about being a "good" person and how "good" people try to keep everyone happy.

Dad didn't push the point. In fact, it seemed a bit odd that he gave in so quickly and graciously as he usually fought a lot harder about such matters. He just quietly said, "Oh well, I'd better let you go then," as if resigning himself to the call others had on me. I remember driving back later that Sunday evening brokenhearted for not staying longer with Dad. It was a real wrench. I left to please somebody else and I felt torn in half by duty and love. It was the last time I saw him alive.

I don't know why, but about two years later I was reflecting on my actions around that last time I saw Dad and suddenly it became crystal clear what the huge *cost* of pleasing someone else was just because I thought I *should* do so, when my real desire was to be with Dad. As this realization hit me, I began shaking all over and I sort of collapsed, emotionally and physically, the way runners do when they finish a marathon. I was emptied, undone, and totally spent. In that moment, I knew that the dutiful way I'd lived my life had come to an end. From that point on, I resolved to never again surrender my integrity.

The next day my son was given the "message."

What I got from my small son's words (which on the face of it might seem a little far-fetched) was that Dad was somehow used as part of an intricate mystery that ended up producing a radical change in me. The impact of our last parting was used as a wake-up call about how I was running my life. It held up a mirror to show me that I had my priorities wrong not just with Dad but probably in a whole lot of other areas too. I needed a jolt like this to make me realize how precious my life, my family, and all of creation really is. Somehow, in some unfathomable way, I think he was "used." Sacrificing those last precious moments with me eventually enabled me to gain a better life. As tough as it was, that parting was a generous spirited gift to me. His words relayed to me via his grandson were his stamp of approval that I had used this gift wisely.

My life really did change after this. I suppose for the first time I started putting the main things first and I became clearer about all of the other crap that had been driving me up until this point. In spite of my in-laws' displeasure, I persuaded my husband and two primary school aged boys that we should leave the city we'd been living in for the last 17 years to return to our "home," a small rural area on an island well off the beaten track.

Everyone thought I was mad as I worked freelance. "After two weeks everyone will forget you up here, you'll be back, you can't survive down there." Well that was seven years ago and it's the best move we ever made. My kids are growing up in this wonderful environment. We bought land my grandmother used to own and our children play football in a park where giant trees planted by my husband's great great grandfather flourish. What a thrill to know that my kids are growing up in the place where their ancestors once lived, and in a weird and wonderful way they are sort of still there looking after all of us. And, wonder of wonders, we now share this pleasure with my in-laws!

I still get lots of work, much of it in new areas that I wouldn't have dreamed of had we not made the move. It was really tough at first and I wondered what on earth I'd done, but now I know it was right as I've come home in so many ways. It's a home-coming of the heart as well as a physical homecoming. Every-thing just seems "right."

I know God had a hand in it. I couldn't prove it or anything like that, but for the last seven years it has seemed like we've been guided by this unseen hand that has cared for us, every-thing just kept slotting into place like it was meant to be. In fact, looking back on my whole life there's been this constant pres-ence. I'm comfortable calling it God. I just know it's God.

— Actress aged 38 at the time of her experience

This final account was one of the most extraordinary related to me. It involved a physical presence performing a life saving role.

During World War II, I served with the RAF as an LAC (lead-ing aircraftman) – half of the time I was seconded to the RAAF. Towards the end of the war with Japan, I was stationed in Singapore. One time on R & R a group of us went on a bus to a local beauty spot called Koti Tingi in Jahore Baru, Malaya. There's a big waterfall there, about 300 feet high coming straight out of the mountainside. It is quite magnificent.

While there, something inveigled me, something motivated me to climb down into the head of this waterfall among the rocks. I don't really know why, because I'm afraid of heights.

Whether it was to prove something to me I don't know, but that's as maybe. Anyway, I climbed down and stood on a rock in the middle of the torrent at the head of the chasm. Suddenly I missed my footing and I slipped into the cataract. I was petrified. I was trying to hang on to the sheer sides of the rock, but I couldn't hang on as the power of the water was tremendous. It was as if someone had hold of both of my legs and they were being pulled and pulled. The water was pouring all over me. I could hardly breathe and I thought I was a goner for if I let go I'd be swept over the waterfall.

As I was struggling, I heard a voice say, "Be still." It was a very authoritative voice, almost like that of a commanding officer: "Be still!" And so I was still. Then the voice (he) said, "If you reach underneath the waterfall, the water's worn away little cups, little shallows, and in the shallows are grains of sand." He then said, "Take your copra" (that's the singlet that was in my hand and that I was hanging on with) "and soak it in the sand to give you adhesion to the rocks that you slipped on."

I tried to rush to do this and again he said, "Be still! Wait until I tell you to move. If you lift your foot about three inches you'll find a little niche in the wall." And he coached me out and bit by bit directed me up the sides of the chasm. I had my eyes shut during this and then I looked up. There was this huge man standing on the rock above me and yet his feet were about six inches off the rock – he was standing there in midair. He had a sort of surplice on and a reddish colored sash down the front of it and a blue cloak behind it. He said, "Peace be with you" or "Pax" or something like that and I lay there gasping for breath.

I looked up and there were about 30 of my chaps (fellow servicemen) all lined up above me. From this position some of them had taken photographs of the whole incident. The photos show me standing on the rock before I fell and clambering out.

But the really odd thing is the photographs taken of me lying exhausted on the rock don't show me at all. I'm not there. Instead there's a sort of charcoal outline of a figure with its arms stretched out as if I'd been transfigured in some way. I don't know, and I can't explain what it is or why this should be so.

Although it all happened over 50 years ago it's as clear as the day it happened. It's never left me – never.

The one conclusion I've made from this and other experiences is that there is a life after death. There must be.

The whole thing transformed my life as much as I now know there are people looking after us if we only listen. Listen to ourselves. If we really really heard what is being said inside ourselves, we'd never be alone.

– Man aged 74

The stories all follow a typical pattern: an extraordinary event resulting in an insight which leads to a re-evaluation or changed life view. Were these anecdotes from another culture, we would have little trouble accepting them, granting them a respect and reverence we would rarely extend to those in our own society. Indeed, a colleague of mine tells of a time she needed filming permission from a Maori community. The elder she spoke to said he'd talk to the ancestors about it. He spent the following 30 hours sitting on top of a hill in the community's graveyard. On his return, he said they had told him it was all right – permission granted. She totally accepted this as a legitimate way of making decisions. I doubt her reaction would be the same were she informed by a business person on the 26th floor of a city tower block that they'd have to pray a few hours about her request for an interview!

We accept other cultures' experiential spirituality because we can see the "logic" behind what they do. Anthropology has suc-

108 — SECRET AFFAIRS OF THE SOUL

cessfully sold the line that there is always a good reason for primitive taboos and religious practices; they stop the tribe from eating poisonous foods, get them through famines, give them hope to carry on when devastated by natural disasters. By contrast, we Westerners, being rational and civilized, don't need such "tricks" to cope with life. So we publicly deny our soul affairs while privately adding them to our register of profound intimacies.

It wasn't always this way. In our own culture up until a century ago, the above anecdote of the drowning airman would have been accepted and put into the experiential religious context that existed at the time. More than likely it would have been described as a saintly or angelic intervention. Even if the church hierarchy didn't condone the divine intervention line, the gentleman would almost certainly have had his peers accept it. Today, where superstition and religion are frequently seen as synonymous, such an experience put into religious language would almost certainly discredit the teller of the tale.

It's not that we have fewer soul affairs than other cultures or previous generations. Things are pretty much the same as they always have been. Indeed, the only difference between the soul affairs of today and yesterday is the language we use to describe them and the vastly different levels of public acceptance they receive.

CHAPTER NINE

ANCIENT AND MODERN

God needs no pointing out to a child.

– Akan proverb from Ghana

There's nothing new about soul affairs. They are as old as the human race, cropping up as they do in all cultures at all times. They are a truly universal phenomenon. Indeed when historical accounts of soul affairs are placed alongside modern experiences some fascinating similarities emerge. Take, for example, the case of a poor shoemaker who one afternoon in 1600 in the small town of Gorlitz on the border of Germany and Poland, found himself staring at a bright pewter dish. The sunlight reflected off it as he looked at it for a quarter of an hour.

I saw and knew more than if I had been many years at a University...the Being of Beings, the Byss and Abyss...the essential nature of evil and of good...The greatness of the triumphing that was in the spirit I cannot express...in this Light my spirit suddenly saw through all, and in and by all the creatures, even in herbs and grass, it knew God – who He is and how He is and what His will is – and suddenly in that Light my will was set on by a mighty impulse to describe the Being of God.[1]

This description was written 12 years after the event by Jacob Boheme (1575–1624) who later became a noted mystic. It bears a remarkable resemblance to my own experience in the mountains when I spontaneously became aware of the "Source," and to that of the man in his early 70s who as a four-year-old boy became "lost" in the bracken. A similar transcendent soul affair was experienced in the 15th century by the founder of the Jesuit order, St. Ignatius of Loyola (1491–1556).

One day St. Ignatius went to pray in a church outside Manresa. The road led along a riverbank. When he sat down to rest, his eyes fixed on the running water and his mind in prayer, he experienced an intense and sudden enlightenment. Although he could never find words to describe what had been revealed to him there, he used to say that all things seemed to have been made new, and that what he understood in that moment exceeded everything that he had learned during his whole life.[2]

Three centuries earlier a German abbess, the first in a great line of women mystics, had this experience.

And it came to pass in the eleven hundred and forty-first year of the incarnation of Jesus Christ, Son of God, when I was forty-two years and seven months old, that the heavens were opened and a blinding light of exceptional brilliance flowed through my entire brain. And so it kindled my whole heart and breast like a flame, not burning but warming...and suddenly I understood the meaning of the expositions of the books, that is to say of the Psalter, the evangelists, and other catholic books of the Old and New Testaments.[3]

– Hildegard of Bingen 1098–1179

We accept that such transcendent soul affairs were the norm for saints and for mystics, for they devoted themselves to seek and commune with God. We have well-kept records of their experiences, preserved either through their own writings or those of their biographers. Undoubtedly, they had many more intensely ecstatic moments and felt the hand of divine guidance on them much more than ordinary people, but they by no means had a monopoly on such moments. There is no reason to suppose that ordinary people in the past had fewer soul affairs than we do today. It's just that, generally, it was only those within a religious context whose experiences were recorded. This natural exclusion of commoners and laity from accounts of religious experience has given the impression that barely any laypeople in the past had soul affairs of much significance.

The manner of writing about the saints and mystics has further compounded this belief. Candid details of their lives have been filtered out, making them appear more holy than human. This has kept in place a sacred distance between them and the sinful masses. It's a pity, because often the saints and mystics were far more like us than we have been led to believe. The popular picture of them as wispy, ethereal, gentle, and meek persons is somewhat misleading. Although undoubtedly many fitted this description, others have had their life stories carefully sanitized concealing their true unaffected and down-to-earth characters. Like many contemporary experiences, their affairs of the soul sometimes came about in circumstances that were none too holy and far removed from any religious setting. However, such details have become blurred, lost or deliberately omitted from the chronicles of their lives. What we are often left with is an extruded, edited version that speaks only of the profound insight gained and that leaves out the really interesting and often very colorful human elements of the story.

For example, St. Ignatius, the son of a Spanish nobleman, was a swashbuckling, rampaging soldier given to fits of pique and temper. Even after his conversion, he once let his mule make the decision whether or not to kill a man who had questioned the virginity of Our Lady. Luckily, the animal made the right choice and the man was spared! While he was defending an ally's city, a cannonball struck Ignatius in the legs, literally stopping him in his tracks. In the months of convalescence that followed this severe injury, he had much time to daydream and muse about the campaigns he would fight and the ladies he would woo. In the absence of any other reading material, he read and re-read two books: one on the life of Christ, the other on the saints of the desert. In his arrogance, he mused upon how he might outdo the holy Desert Fathers in their austerity and piety. From such audacious notions emerged a profound insight. A stunning moment of clarity, an affair of the soul. When Ignatius contemplated the secular world of campaigns and conquests, he noticed that he was left feeling empty, hollow, and incomplete. On the other hand, when musing on outdoing the saints, he would emerge from his contemplations cheerful, reassured, and optimistic. This awareness became the basis of his spiritual exercises, which have helped millions to discern the spiritual effect thoughts have on our moods, personalities, and activities.

Were I to read only the theology behind St. Ignatius's insight, I would have trouble relating to it. Knowing more about the man and the soul affair that precipitated such wisdom helps me to understand. I can relate to it because this unexpurgated account is very human and entirely plausible. I like this saint; he's my kind of guy.

Hildegard, too, was no airy, removed mystic. Although physically small, she possessed remarkable energy. She founded two

convents; was a poet and a musician (over 60 hymns are attributed to her); wrote a long treatise in nine books (one being a complete guide to the nature and properties of herbs); was skilled in
medicine, deeply interested in politics, and kept up a solid corre-
spondence with the greatest men of her day – whom she often
rebuked for perceived faults! Her motivation and source of energy came from her inward commands and visions. "Living Light"
was her name for God, while that within her was "The Shade of
the Living Light."

From my infancy until now, in the 70th year of my age…my
soul has always beheld this Light; and in it my soul soars to
the summit of the firmament and into a different air…The
brightness which I see is not limited by space and is more brilliant than the radiance round the sun…Within that brightness I
sometimes see another light, for which the name Lux Vivens has
been given me. When and how I see this, I cannot tell; but sometimes when I see it all sadness and pain is lifted from me, and I
seem a simple girl again, and an old woman no more![4]

Hildegard's accounts touch on a theme that weaves a common
thread through soul affairs both ancient and modern; that of fire
and light. The accountant in the previous chapter who sensed
his family disintegrating found, like Hildegard, that such light led
to comfort, peace, understanding, and knowledge. Here from
more than a century ago, is Richard M. Bucke's account of his
own fire-like religious experience.

—◉—

I had spent the evening in a great city, with two friends, reading and discussing poetry and philosophy. We parted at midnight. I had a long drive in a hansom to my lodging. My mind, deeply under the influence of the ideas, images, and emotions called up by the reading and talk, was calm and peaceful. I was in a state of quiet, almost passive enjoyment, not actually thinking, but letting ideas, images, and emotions flow of themselves, as it were, through my mind. All at once, without warning of any kind, I found myself wrapped in a flame-coloured cloud. For an instant I thought of fire, an immense conflagration somewhere close by in that great city; the next, I knew that the fire was within myself. Directly afterward there came upon me a sense of exultation, of immense joyousness accompanied or immediately followed by an intellectual illumination impossible to describe. Among other things, I did not merely come to believe, but I saw that the universe is not composed of dead matter, but is, on the contrary, a living Presence; I became conscious in myself of eternal life. It was not a conviction that I would have eternal life, but a consciousness that I possessed eternal life then; I saw that all men are immortal; that the cosmic order is such that without any peradventure all things work together for the good of each and all; that the foundation principle of the world, of all the worlds, is what we call love, and that the happiness of each and all is in the long run absolutely certain. The vision lasted a few seconds and was gone; but the memory of it and the sense of the reality of what it taught have remained during the quarter of a century which has since elapsed. I knew that what the vision showed was true. I had attained to a point of view from which I saw that it must be true. That view, that conviction, I may say that consciousness, has never, even during periods of the deepest depression, been lost.[5]

This fire and light experience is not only found today and in previous centuries, it is a common experience spanning millennia. There are many biblical stories that recount fire-like soul affairs: Moses encountered the burning bush, Elisha prayed for his servant's eyes to be opened and this menial follower suddenly saw "hills full of horses and chariots of fire all around Elisha."[6] Christ's disciples on the day of Pentecost "saw what seemed to be tongues of fire that separated and came to rest on each of them."[7] Certainly Bucke's description is in no way dissimilar to that of St. Alonso, a 16th-century Spanish monastery doorkeeper.

Once, when St. Alonso was engaged in earnestly praying that he might be granted joy in suffering and love his persecutors, he had the following experience: Suddenly, before he realised what was happening, there came upon him a sort of fiery comet, like those which fall from heaven at night. It came down on him from on high and wounded him in the side so that it left his heart on fire with love for his neighbour. And it seemed to him that he could not wish ill towards his neighbour, even if he were to do the most terrible things to him.[8]

Such transcendent fiery soul affairs, although occurring centuries and continents apart, are strikingly similar. The same holds true for other types of soul affairs. Although the language may differ and the settings may change, soul affairs equivalent to our modern experiences can be found popping up throughout the world during all periods of history.

Some of the earliest recorded soul affairs come from the Indian subcontinent before 2000 BCE. The Mandukya Upanishads speak of a state of consciousness beyond dreamless sleep that is "unperceived...incomprehensible...unthinkable...all peace..."[9] The Greek philosopher Socrates (469–399 BCE) spoke of the small inner voice, but doubted anyone else ever heard it. However, the oldest soul affair I've come across from an ordinary everyday person is an account written 3,500–3,900 years ago. It's from the Hebrew Book of Genesis and like so many contemporary accounts occurs during a particularly traumatic life event. In many ways it reads like a modern TV soap opera.

The principal characters are the elderly patriarch of a nomadic tribe, his wife, and her maid. The couple was childless. So desperate were they for progeny that they engaged in an early version of surrogate parenting, whereby the husband, with the wife's consent, sleeps with the maid. This way they figure there's a much better chance of a child. Accordingly the maid moves in with the husband and in due course conceives. The now pregnant and very smug maid flaunts her fecundity in the wife's face. Naturally the wife takes exception to this and with the husband on side turns on the maid, making her life a living hell. The maid puts up with this for a while until it finally gets to be too much and she quits camp. The problem is, there's really nowhere to go as they're already in the middle of a desert.

In many ways, it's a suicide mission – the odds of a pregnant young woman surviving alone in the rugged inhospitable wilderness are not high. Vulnerable, abandoned, uncared-for, outcast, dejected, presumably in deep despair, defenseless against any passerby who might wish to ravage her, the poor maid wanders about desperately afraid. At some stage, I imagine she simply gives up, for there appears to be absolutely no hope. Perhaps broken and sobbing on the ground, totally at the end of her rope, something unexpected happens – a divine presence, "The Angel of the Lord" appears.

The angel tells her various things, one being to go back to her masters. What's interesting, though, is that when she relates her story, her description is not of an angel, but of God, whom she identifies as the "God who sees me." "I have now seen the one who sees me."[10] There has been some suggestion, in fact, that the word "angel" might be a later insertion by Hebrew censors anxious to stamp out any suggestion that Yahweh was in the habit of conversing with common mortals.[11] In any event, the Torah translates her saying, "You Are El Roi," which means, "You are the God of seeing." She continues by saying, "Have I not gone on seeing after He saw me!"

The God who sees me.

Living in a highly sophisticated, technologically advanced civilization, it's hard to imagine a culture more removed from ours than the nomadic tribe in which this peasant girl lived over three millennia ago. Yet the sense of the presence of God or power she conveys bypasses the angel insertion of the censors and thousands of years of history to resonate with anyone who at any time has experienced a transcendent affair of the soul. In so many accounts of modern-day soul affairs, it is this being "known," this being "seen" to the very depths of our souls that distinguishes the experience from anything else we've ever felt. The following comments are from a random selection of contemporary accounts.

I was getting information from my deepest parts…

I felt I was "me" at my purest level…

I had no doubts, I wasn't surprised, I just knew...

I was totally and utterly transparent, my innermost core exposed, yet I sensed no disapproval, only an overwhelming sense of support...

I felt as if everything around me was ancient and I was part of it...

It was a wonderful feeling, a complete takeover, yet I was still me!

I just know that this – whatever it was – was what had created me, was there at the beginning of me, others, the world, everything.

The literature of the religious traditions records an abundance of soul affairs. It is often such powerful experiences that established the religion in the first place: for Judaism, it was Abraham, Isaac, and Moses hearing and obeying Yahweh; Gautama's enlightenment under the bodhi tree spawned Buddhism; Jesus of Nazareth seems to have enjoyed a remarkable intimacy with the God of Israel, whom he confidently called *Abba* (Daddy). The archangel Gabriel appeared many times to Muhammad in the mountains behind Mecca and dictated to him the contents of the Qur'an. From Noah's ark building and David's Goliath slaying to the shepherds following an angel's directions to a Bethlehem stable, our Western religious tradition is full of reports of ancients who felt guided by seen and unseen presences they attributed to God.

When I put our modern-day accounts alongside the biblical stories and the religious experiences of the mystics and saints, I can only conclude that we are all talking about the same thing, albeit in a language appropriate and unique to the culture, customs, and context of the time. In the past, our English speaking Western culture would have more often than not assumed that a soul affair was "God" or "of God." Nowadays, with institutionalized religion playing a far smaller part in our lives, there is a much greater reluctance to jump to a divine conclusion. Even so, it is not hard to see we're describing the same experiences our ancestors had.

In 1997, a team of neuroscientists from the University of California in San Diego released the results of a study they had done on a group of epileptics who had reported having intense mystical episodes during seizures. When the epileptics were shown words invoking spiritual beliefs, a circuit of nerves in their frontal lobes became electrically active. The scientists also tested a group of non-epileptics who described themselves as intensely religious. When shown the trigger words, they too exhibited a noticeable difference in the electrical activity of their frontal lobes, more so than a control group of non-religious people who were given the same stimulus. The circuit of nerves was nicknamed the "God spot." Evolutionary scientists have suggested that such a "God spot" in our frontal lobes might well be a Darwinian adaptation to encourage individuals in society to cooperate through common religious beliefs. Religious experts suggest it makes perfect sense for God to create in us a physical point of connection to him/herself.[12]

Whatever the explanation, we seem to be biologically hard-wired for transcendent spiritual or religious moments – soul affairs. Such a biological predisposition would certainly explain why all societies recognize a fundamental "oneness" whether it be Tao (Taoism), Allah (Islam), Suchness (Buddhism), God (Christianity), Yahweh (Judaism), Brahman (Hinduism), Wakan Tanka

(Native American tradition)[13] or Ra (Ancient Egyptian). Within the various religions, it is the described encounters with this "oneness" that resonate so clearly with modern-day accounts of ordinary, everyday Westerners. Surely we're all talking about the same thing? The following story puts it into perspective.

Once a man went into a wood and saw an animal on a tree. He came back and told another man he had seen an animal with a beautiful red colour on a certain tree. The second man said: "When I went into the woods I saw that animal. But why do you call it red? It's green." Another man who was there contradicted them both and said it was yellow. Then others arrived and they began to argue, some saying it was grey, violet, blue and so on.

To settle the argument they all went to the tree. They saw a man sitting under it. When they asked him, he said: "Yes, I live under this tree and I know the animal very well. You are all correct. Sometimes it appears red, or green – violet, grey or blue. It's a chameleon. Sometimes it has no colour at all."

In the same way, somebody who constantly thinks of God knows his nature. He can reveal himself to others in various forms and aspects. Then again, sometimes God has attributes, sometimes he has none. Only the man who lives under the tree knows this. The others suffer from the agony of futile argument.[14]

– Ramakrishna (1833–1886)

Transcendent soul affairs are an integral part of most if not all religious traditions. Zen Buddhists lay total emphasis on direct experience to attain "oneness." Quakers maintain that words and doctrine just get in the way and so wait together in silence to hear God speak. The Gnostics, too, thought scriptures and doctrines to be of little value compared to direct contact with God and spent their time in the desert seeking it. Moslems expect to have at least one direct encounter with God in their lifetime. Today, there are many in all religions who live separate from the world, communing daily with the divine. It is an integral and accepted part of religious tradition. But these are people who deliberately set out to seek and commune with God. How infinitely more intriguing when a presence or power seemingly takes the initiative and without invitation dramatically penetrates ordinary people.

Western holy scriptures contain many accounts of soul affairs happening to ordinary people, but often the person is so changed by their experience they eventually become an outstanding religious figure: Joseph, left for dead by his brothers, ends up becoming a powerful Egyptian nobleman; Mary, told by the archangel Gabriel that she will give birth to the "son of the most high," is instantly catapulted from obscurity to near divinity; Saul, persecuting those who follow "The Way," is thrown from his horse, temporarily blinded, and hears a voice. He becomes St. Paul, the most prominent Christian proselytizer, without whom the religion may never have grown beyond a small messianic sect. Such dramatic events help establish the notion that if God enters your life you will be propelled on to religious center stage. People who have God intervene in their lives but who don't go on to build an ark or lead their people out of slavery are rarely heard from again. This gives the impression that our soul affairs cannot be from the same source as those of religious heroes, for records of divine intervention, after which an ordinary person continues on with their mundane life, are not nearly as well known.

Yet there are many such scriptural records of soul affairs happening to "nobodies": Samuel's mother, who becomes fertile at God's intervention, is thereafter mentioned only briefly; the woman at the well, who first recognizes Christ as the Messiah, soon disappears; the many diseased, ailing, and ill that Jesus and his disciples healed, quickly vanish. All these historical figures have dramatic soul affairs, but they soon fade into obscurity.

Similarly, we seldom hear of the countless soul affairs that occur every day in our modern world. They are not the stuff of headlines, and because they are so intensely personal and intimate they are rarely talked about. They are hidden from public view in the same way that good deeds are. As writer Peggy Noonan says, "Most people aren't appreciated enough, and the bravest things we do in our lives are usually known only to ourselves. No one throws ticker tape on the man who chose to be faithful to his wife, or the lawyer who didn't take the drug money, or the daughter who held her tongue again and again. All this anonymous heroism."[15]

My hairdresser has quite a few elderly clients who make appointments to have their hair done two or three times a week, not because their hair needs attention, but simply because they need to be touched and talked to. The salon only takes payment once every few weeks, which is when these women would normally have their hair done. Very few know of this wonderful kindness. Out of sight is out of mind. And yet I'm sure there are millions of such wonderful acts of altruism performed every day. In the same way, because we seldom hear of ordinary people's soul affairs, only the divine encounters of outstanding biblical proportions are considered to be spiritually legitimate.

However, this assumption was first called into question almost a century ago. William James's *Varieties of Religious Experience* is still, almost 100 years on, one of the most extensive texts on the topic. James could comfortably use the label "religious experience" without striking the sort of problems people nowadays have with such a term, for up until a few generations ago our ancestors were familiar with Bible characters and passages of scripture. Concepts such as sin, heaven, hell, and prayer, sat comfortably within mainstream public opinion, so James's accounts frequently mention God as a self-evident given. The divinity, of course, was always referred to as male.

I was in perfect health: we were on our sixth day of tramping, and in good training. We had come the day before from Sixt to Trient by Buet. I felt neither fatigue, hunger, nor thirst, and my state of mind was equally healthy. I had had at Forlaz good news from home; I was subject to no anxiety, either near or remote, for we had a good guide, and there was not a shadow of uncertainty about the road we should follow. I can best describe the condition in which I was by calling it a state of equilibrium. When all at once I experienced a feeling of being raised above myself, I felt the presence of God – I tell of the thing just as I was conscious of it – as if his goodness and his power were penetrating me altogether. The throb of emotion was so violent that I could barely tell the boys to pass on and not wait for me. I then sat down on a stone, unable to stand any longer, and my eyes overflowed with tears. I thanked God that in the course of my life he had taught me to know him, that he sustained my life and took pity both on the insignificant creature and on the sinner that I was. I begged him ardently that my life might be consecrated to the doing of his will, I felt his reply, which was that I should do his will from day to day, in humility and poverty, leaving him, the Almighty God, to be judge of whether I should some time be called to bear witness more conspicuously. Then, slowly, the ecstasy left my heart; that is, I felt that God had withdrawn the communion which he had granted, and I was able to walk on, but very slowly, so strongly was I still possessed by the interior emotion. Besides, I had wept uninterruptedly for several minutes, my eyes were swollen, and I did not wish my companions to see me. The state of ecstasy may have lasted four or five minutes, although it seemed at the time to last much longer. My comrades waited for me ten minutes at the cross of Barine, but I took about twenty-five or thirty minutes to join them, for as well as I can remember, they said that I had kept them back for about half an hour. The impression had been so profound that in climbing slowly the slope I asked myself if it were possible that Moses on Sinai could have had a more intimate communication with God. I think it well to add that in this ecstasy of mine God had neither form, color, odor, nor taste; moreover, that the feeling of his presence was accompanied with no determinate localization. It was rather as if my personality had been transformed by the presence of a spiritual spirit. But the more I seek words to express this intimate intercourse, the more I feel the impossibility of describing the thing by any of our usual images. At bottom the expression most apt to render what I felt is this: God was present, though invisible; he fell under no one of my senses, yet my consciousness perceived him.[16]

– Man late 19th century

Although James put on the record that ordinary people experienced soul affairs, he could not comment on how widespread they were. That had to wait for the social surveying techniques of the late 20th century.

However, he did make a key observation about religious experiences that has proven consistent. Despite what label is applied to them and where they occur, the experiences have a conviction quotient second to none. The recipient is absolutely adamant that what they have experienced is one of the truest, most real experiences of their lives. It appears that just one glimpse of paradise in a person's lifetime may be all the convincing an individual ever needs. Regarding the convincing nature of the experiences, James noted,

They are as convincing to those who have them as any direct sensible experiences can be, and they are, as a rule, much more convincing than results established by mere logic ever are. One may indeed be entirely without them; probably more than one of you here present is without them in any marked degree; but if you do have them, and have them at all strongly, the probability is that you cannot help regarding them as genuine perceptions of truth, as revelations of a kind of reality which no adverse argument, however unanswerable by you in words, can expel from your belief.[17]

I remember the night, and almost the very spot on the hilltop, where my soul opened out, as it were, into the Infinite, and there was a rushing together of the two worlds, the inner and the outer. It was deep calling unto deep – the deep that my own struggle had opened up within being answered by the unfathomable deep without, reaching beyond the stars. I stood alone with Him who had made me, and all the beauty of the world, and love, and sorrow, and even temptation. I did not seek Him, but felt the perfect unison of my spirit with His. The ordinary sense of things around me faded. For the moment nothing but an ineffable joy and exaltation remained. It is impossible fully to describe the experience. It was like the effect of some great orchestra when all the separate notes have melted into one swelling harmony that leaves the listener conscious of nothing save that his soul is being wafted upwards, and almost bursting with its own emotion. The perfect stillness of the night was thrilled by a more solemn silence. The darkness held a presence that was all the more felt because it was not seen. I could not any more have doubted that He was there than that I was. Indeed, I felt myself to be, if possible, the less real of the two.

My highest faith in God and truest idea of him were then born in me. I have stood upon the Mount of Vision since, and felt the Eternal round about me. But never since has there come quite the same stirring of the heart. Then, if ever, I believe, I stood face to face with God, and was born anew of his spirit. There was, as I recall it, no sudden change of thought or of belief, except that my early crude conception had, as it were, burst into flower. There was no destruction of the old, but a rapid, wonderful unfolding. Since that time no discussion that I have heard of the proofs of God's existence has been able to shake my faith. Having once felt the presence of God's spirit, I have never lost it again for long. My most assuring evidence of his existence is deeply rooted in that hour of vision, in the memory of that supreme experience, and in the conviction, gained from reading and reflection, that something the same has come to all who have found God. I am aware that it may justly be called mystical. I am not enough acquainted with philosophy to defend it from that or any other charge. I feel that in writing of it I have overlaid it with words rather than put it clearly to your thought. But, such as it is, I have described it as carefully as I now am able to do."[18]

– Clergyman late 19th century

In presenting these historical accounts, my aim has been to point out the consistent nature and frequency of soul affairs across time and culture, for even in these information rich times there would be few who would suspect just how prolific they are and have always been. I believe it is extremely important to put this on the record, for the convincing nature of the experiences combined with the lack of any well-known objective information on the commonality of soul affairs has led to some very public uses and abuses of them. If there was a greater awareness of how normal these experiences are, there would be less chance that a small minority would erroneously assume their soul affair gives them special authority. There would also be less chance they could gather around themselves a band of devout followers willing to blindly believe and obey their orders, even to commit murder and suicide.

CHAPTER TEN

POWER, EVIL, AND CONTROL

Psychic powers without humility and without the guiding insights of spirituality will lead astray even more fatally than material powers, similarly unguided, are doing at present.

– Aldous Huxley writing to Thomas Merton[1]

One of the most abused aspects of soul affairs occurs when individuals take it upon themselves to use their experience to operate amorally. Being ignorant of how common their experience is, a few assume they have been divinely favored to take on the mantle of a demigod. Jim Jones's horror in the jungles of Guyana, where in 1978 more than 900 men, women, and children of the People's Temple cult killed themselves with poisoned drinks; David Koresh's bloody stand at Waco, Texas; and, more recently, the horrific slaughter in Uganda of followers of The Movement for the Restoration of the Ten Commandments of God, show how far unchecked messianic convictions can go. Yitzhak Rabin, winner of the Nobel Peace Prize for his efforts to make peace with the Palestinian Liberation Organization, met his end at the hands of a fellow Israeli who was convinced God had given him divine license to assassinate the man who had made peace with the en-

130 — SECRET AFFAIRS OF THE SOUL

emy. Whether or not Adolf Hitler ever had a soul affair I don't know but one of the more chilling quotes I came across was from one of his 1936 Reichstag speeches: "Today, I believe that I am acting in accordance with the will of the Almighty Creator: by defending myself against the Jew, I am fighting for the work of the Lord."[2]

There are other examples that stop short of mass murder, but which are still highly damaging. Many leaders have used a perceived spiritual advantage to leverage themselves into positions for corrupt ends, such as the now infamous televangelists Jimmy Swaggart and Jim Bakker, and New Age guru Shree Bhagwan Rajneesh, who, as well as owning a bevy of Rolls Royces, had purposely built orgy rooms on his property in Oregon.

In their book, *The Five Stages of the Soul* [3] authors Harry Moody and David Carroll suggest a good rule of thumb is to "run like hell" if the spiritual leader or the guide of the movement is having sexual relations with group members or is making excessive monetary demands. As regards the group as a whole, they caution that it would be wise to steer clear if it puts unjustified emphasis on power, or jeopardizes the health and welfare of its members.

In the overwhelming majority of soul affairs, however, humility not arrogance is the norm. Sir Alister Hardy discovered that most people found the idea of being especially chosen quite repugnant and rejected it out of hand. If anything, people tended to underreport times when they experienced a guiding hand, as it might look like they were claiming divine purpose. Indeed, a deep natural modesty seemed to be the rule rather than the exception. In a personal conversation, someone once told Hardy that although he had a strong feeling his life was somehow arranged he dared not bring himself to believe it was true because "such a belief would imply the appalling presumption that he could be the object of preferential treatment."[4]

Another common misunderstanding regarding soul affairs is that evil presences or powers are just as likely to be encountered as benign ones. Confrontations between the forces of evil and the power of good are the basic ingredient of fairy tales and fables. Ancient myths and legends abound with stories of sorcery, witchcraft, imps, monsters, and evil spirits. With such a folklore of evil, it could be assumed that sinister attacks and visitations might also occur in today's world. Certainly the volume of tales from the dark side that fill our TV and movie screens could easily lead us to believe that they might not be a particularly unusual occurrence. Yet the actual recorded incidence of those who have experienced a presence or power in everyday life that was described as evil or non-benign is relatively low. Consistent with the British survey results, only a few of the several hundred accounts I came across mentioned anything along these lines.

My first experience that I would place in this area occurred in late 1991. I was living with my father and stepmother at the time. I had retired to my bed for the night, falling asleep around 11 p.m. I was awakened by the sound of something fairly light, like a golf ball, dropping onto the carpeted floor, seemingly near my bedroom. It was around 2 a.m. by my alarm clock. While I was still considering what had made the noise that woke me, I was absolutely sent into shock by what I'd describe as the sound of a rasping, hissing male voice, growling out the obscenity "F— OFF." The voice seemed to come from just above my head, as I lay on my pillow. I was petrified. My mind reeled, desperately scanning itself for logical explanations and reassurances. I was so scared that I picked up a pair of nearby earphones and actually bent them in half to make a makeshift weapon to defend myself. They were the kind with a metal piece joining the earphones.

This is an indication of how real the noise sounded to me. I wasn't sure that it didn't come from inside my room. Strangely, though, I could sense no other indications of a physical presence in our house. After about ten minutes I felt safe enough to get up and I slowly looked around the dark house. Thankfully, I found nothing and eventually went back to sleep. When I got up the next day, I asked my parents if they'd heard anything like it the previous night, as their room is next to mine. They had not.

It was most unexpected, just like a bolt out of the blue. I mean, who expects something like this if they're lying down in bed to have some sleep! I was in absolute tranquillity. I had had a normal day at work. It was just so clear and vivid. I was fully awake and "it" just ripped through me like talons.

At this stage I asked the young man to give me an impression of what "it" sounded like. He asked for a moment to center himself, to recall the exact tone, and then the back of my neck prickled as a hissing, rasping exclamation came down the phone line. Later he described the rasping as being like cats fighting – that was one of the explanations he mentally checked out. Could there have been a cat fight outside the window? Perhaps there was another explanation.

Indeed, after the fear factor had subsided I became quite excited and intrigued about this experience. I'd been involved in something special. After about 10 to 15 minutes, I wasn't scared and I started looking for a physical explanation.

Curiously, around the time of this I was counseling a client who was involved with a satanic cult. Myself and several other counselors were involved with the client for several months and I had had threats, indirectly, to pull my head back in, so to speak, through this client. I'm not saying this was a psychic attack, but it is an interesting fact, I think.

– Man aged 21

One of the problems with accounts such as this is identifying the presence or power that was experienced. Most of us are comfortable attributing our transcendent moments, answers to prayer, and experiences of an unseen guiding hand, to "God" or to a benign presence or power. But what is one to make of a case like this? Should we wish to check it out there is a very limited repertoire of help to call on. Standard psychiatric and psychological practice would first probe our state of mind, something those of us who are perfectly sane would not wish to put ourselves through, as mistakes can sometimes be made with professional diagnoses! We could try talking with a priest, but few of us have a user-friendly cleric on tap. Basically we're pretty much on our own because there are few trustworthy spiritual guides who would seriously and thoughtfully consider our experience.

This being the case I offer the following quick discernment guide to help establish where our experiences may come from. I've used this spiritual rule of thumb for many years. It is based on commonly accepted theological principles and has stood me in good stead when I've tried to place my experiences in context.

If our experience is from God or a benevolent presence or power, then it will most likely be peaceful, consistent, loving, patient, uplifting, instructive, comforting, clear, kind, welcoming of scrutiny, and seldom needing to be responded to in a hurry. On the other hand, if our experience is confusing, promotes fear and panic, rejects scrutiny, produces guilt, creates anxiety, is pushy or urgent and accusatory then it may well be from the spiritual realms, but not the benign ones. If our experience appeals to our egos or will make us look good in front of others, then its origin is most likely to be found within ourselves. This is why I believe it is wise to reject those who use their experiences for self-aggrandizement, power, or profit.

Unless we're dabbling with the occult, it is highly unlikely our soul affairs will match horror movie evil visitations. What's far more probable is that we may be aware of an inner voice or a guiding hand, but because of a personal agenda we will fail to give it the attention it deserves. American writer Tobias Wolff, quoted in John Cornwell's book *The Hiding Places of God*, explores this puzzling but very human trait in the following account.[5]

I don't see well. It's a condition I've always resented. As a boy I wouldn't even admit to it until I began to suffer from headaches, and could no longer read the blackboards at school. I hated my glasses and wore them only upon necessity, walking around most of the time in a blur, as if under water. Later I tried contact lenses but my eyes wouldn't tolerate them. Anyway, they made me feel like a fraud. What I really wanted was perfect vision.

I mention this by way of preamble to a story about something that happened to me in the summer of 1972, during a pilgrimage to Lourdes. But first I should explain how I got there.

At my mother's wish I was baptised a Catholic at the age of ten, but faith, conscious faith, played no part in my life until I was in my twenties.

That's not true. It did play a part in my life, an active part, because I was vigilantly suspicious of it, understanding instinc-

tively that it would subvert the plans I had for myself, merce-
nary, vainglorious as most of those plans were. And I believed
that faith would somehow blind me, keep me from seeing things
clearly. Certainly it would change me. I was afraid of it. I went
on being afraid of it, go on being afraid of it even now, years
after it entered my life irrevocably.

In my twenties, as I said, faith became a possibility for
me. Why then? I can think of reasons. But reasons don't, in
the end, explain faith any more than they can create it. Something happened, an inward turning, a sense of being both
cornered and upheld. But even in this turning I felt a sense of
reluctance and doubt.

In the summer of 1972 I went to Lourdes for a week. I lived
in a barracks with other men. We weren't there very much – only
to eat and sleep. The rest of our time was given over to performing different services for the sick, to whom Lourdes is dedicated.
We worked in the dining halls, in the hospitals, in the baths –
wherever we were needed. I worked mostly at the baths,
volunteering again and again because the experience was
strange, and harrowing, and therefore, I thought, good for me.

Good health makes provincials of us; we take the border
between ourselves and the unhealthy as ordained, fitting, and
eternal, and do not give much thought to what lies on the other
side. At the baths I was, at least for a time, shaken out of this
provincialism.

There were four of us in each bathing pool. Our task was to
receive the men and boys who were brought in to us and to separate them from their wheelchairs and braces and walkers, then
undress them and carry them into the water, where we prayed
over them. I saw the human body under every kind of attack. It
was good to recognize that hope and faith and even joy, could
live on in such ruins. But the experience also appalled me, and

I was not displeased to be taken out of the baths one afternoon and driven with some other volunteers to the local airport where we were to help a group of disabled Italian pilgrims embark for the plane ride home.

It was a hot muggy day. The heat hung over the tarmac in a haze that made the light harsh, almost blinding. At first things went smoothly. We wheeled a number of people out to the plane, where they were taken up a ramp by crews of nurses and medics. Then there was a mix-up. They told us to wait at the bottom of the ramp. We waited for a time, and then, outrageously, someone shut the airplane door.

I was with a little girl about two years old. She was completely paralyzed, and had tubes in her nostrils that drained into bags under the sheet that covered her. She looked up at me calmly, too calmly somehow; I couldn't tell whether she heard me or not when I murmured to her in what I hoped was an encouraging tone. I moved her gurney into the shade of the fuselage and fanned her face with my hand. Still they kept us waiting. Then the flies discovered her. I couldn't keep them off, no matter how hard I tried. They swarmed on her face, over her lips, around her eyes. I kept brushing at them but they came right back, humming, persistent. I became desperate with anger. My anger went beyond the situation. It was fundamental, unreasonable; it had to do with the scheme of things. By the time they opened the airplane door again I was weeping, though only I knew it – by now all our faces were flushed and glistening with sweat.

The little girl was with the last group of passengers. After the plane took off I got on a bus back to Lourdes, and it came to me along the way that something peculiar was happening. I had taken my glasses off earlier in the afternoon because they kept slipping down. They were still in my pocket, but I could see as well as if l had them on, could read license plates and make out the features of people we passed, see sheep grazing in distant fields. I couldn't understand it. I squinted and blinked and rubbed my eyes, thinking it must be a lens formed by sweat and tears, but it didn't go away. I felt giddy and restless, happy but uncomfortable, not myself at all. Then I had the distinct thought that when we got back to Lourdes I should go to the grotto and pray. That was all. Go to the grotto and pray.

But I didn't do that. The bus let me off at the barracks and I went inside for a moment to cool off, and fell into conversation with an Irishman I'd gotten to know. He was sharp and honest and very funny. We sat down on his cot and talked, and all the while I was aware of what I wasn't doing and what I wasn't telling him. I had no reason not to mention what had happened – he would have been keenly interested, not at all derisive – but I didn't say a thing about it. We talked and laughed for a couple of hours, then went to dinner, and I never made it to the grotto that day. Next morning I was wearing my glasses again.

Later I told this story to a priest I knew, Father Michael Hollings, and he said, "Oh ye of little faith." He said it with a smile, but he meant it.

What happened? Possibly it was, as I first suspected, a film on my eyes. Possibly it was an illusion – I only thought I was seeing clearly. It would seem ungenerous, un-Godly, to make such a gift conditional, and to take it back. Of course there's no way of knowing what really happened, or what would have happened if I'd gone to the grotto that afternoon.

What interests me now is why I didn't go. I felt, to be sure, some incredulity. But this wasn't the reason. I have a weakness for good company, good talk, but that wasn't it either. That was only a convenient distraction. At heart, I must not have wanted this thing to happen. I don't know why, but I have suspicions. I suspect that I considered myself unworthy of such a gift. And if

I had secured it, what then? I would have had to give up those doubts by which I defined myself, in the world's terms, as a free man. By giving up doubt, I would have lost that measure of pure self-interest to which I felt myself entitled by doubt. Doubt was my connection to the world, to the faithless self in whom I took refuge when faith got hard. Imagine the responsibility of losing. What then? No wonder I was afraid of this gift, afraid of seeing so well.

This story of a "reverse miracle" or a bypassed soul affair highlights a key human trait, which underpins so much of our behavior: we fear that which is out of our control. We fear the unknown, being a victim, pain, sickness and death, going hungry, losing respect. We fear, like Tobias Wolff, having to try something so new and so different that we would have to completely rearrange our way of seeing ourselves and the world. To take such a risk would be a brave step indeed, because in abandoning the familiar we become cut off from our former selves, hopelessly adrift, deeply insecure, and emotionally homeless. Consequently most people would prefer to fail by orthodox means rather than risk success through unorthodox approaches. Fear is one of the reasons why we defy logic and continue to choose the devils we know. After years of traveling with our personal demons, we think we can manage them. Our familiarity with them makes us feel safe.

For years I covered up an embarrassing shyness by "interviewing" people whenever I was in an unfamiliar social situation. If I asked questions, no one had a chance to penetrate my outer shell. Few could see that it was a ruse as they were so busy talking about themselves in response to my interrogation that I escaped scrutiny and avoided embarrassment. Once I acquired these skills I was no longer afraid of uncontrolled social situations. Indeed, I now preferred places full of people I didn't know, for it gave me an opportunity to "work the room" without having to answer anyone else's inquiries. But feeling socially in control came at a price. My proactive questions meant I seldom got a chance to connect with others. It was a terribly lonely existence, for although I spent many evenings busily listening and talking I usually came away feeling hollow and empty.

This very human trait, the seeking of safety through control, profoundly influences the way we run our physical, emotional and spiritual lives. It is why some of us choose to deny, bury, or forget our soul affairs, and like Tobias Wolff, pursue "safer," more concrete spiritual paths that we can control and manage ourselves. Let's briefly look at the psychology behind this need to be in charge of our circumstances.

When we are *doing* something, anything, it increases our feeling of being empowered and safe. When we think we are in charge of our affairs, we feel infinitely more secure and protected than when we are innocent victims of circumstance. Whether we're *actually* in charge or not doesn't matter. Statistically, flying in a commercial airliner is hundreds of times safer than driving a motor vehicle. Yet most of us are much more afraid of flying than we are of driving. When we hold the steering wheel we feel safe, because we are in control. As a passenger on an airplane, we are powerless. This is one of the reasons we demand that regulations to ensure competent pilots and safe aircraft are much more stringent than those for private motorists.

When it comes to soul affairs, there are some interesting parallels. In the same way that we feel safer when driving ourselves, we will always feel far more comfortable with our own soul affairs than the affairs of others. Because we have intimately experienced our own affair, we know it is true and real. On the other hand, we are likely to be nervous of the unpredictable and out of control nature of others' soul affairs. We can never intimately know what someone else has experienced and so we will tend to be wary of it. This reticence to openly endorse each others' experiences is yet another reason why soul affairs remain secret.

One of the ways we reduce our fear in our emotional and physical lives is through taking control. This is why we want to drive the car; it is why we want to earn more money, gain a higher rank, seek accolades and prestige, gain a higher position in our workplace or community, pursue knowledge. Simply being able to mount an argument, argue a case eloquently, or get across our point of view will give us a psychological sense of control.

This quest to control our circumstances is just as influential in the spiritual arena. Although most of our experiences of God or a presence or power are positive, they are random. We can't manufacture or induce them and this produces a certain amount of unease. We're not quite sure what to do. Since action alleviates our dis-ease, we start taking some practical steps. As with our emotional and physical lives, the harder we work at our spirituality, the more effort we put in, the higher our feelings of spiritual confidence. This opens us up to abuse and exploitation.

I began this chapter with some horrifying examples, but often the abuse is more subtle as it comes from within.

In 1980, God touched my life. My 18-month-old son had fallen down our front steps and was knocked unconscious. X-rays showed a fracture right across his skull and I was just so scared something would happen to him. Over the next few days we could feel his head becoming squishy as brain fluid leaked out. We were warned that any further bump could result in serious brain damage or death. I was really scared and had no idea of what to do. A few days after the fall, quite coincidentally, a stranger called around home to pick up some bedding a friend had left a few months earlier. It turned out he was a visiting preacher who offered to pray for my son. He did this and I tell you I was praying too! At that stage, I was just so desperate I'd try anything. That weekend I went to church and went forward. I made a public commitment to God. I didn't care how foolish or stupid I looked, I would've done anything if it meant my son would be healed.

It was amazing really. That day I felt a great burden lift off me. Something changed. It was just so wonderful I can't really describe it, but I knew it was real. The next day when we took our son back to the hospital there was no trace of the fracture, he was completely healed, a complete miracle! It was a fantastic experience and I thought, "If this is Christianity, I'm going to grab it and go with it with both hands." I floated around for a few days and eventually I came down, but my desire to follow God didn't diminish. I thought, "Yes, I've had a taste, I want to go with this, I want all that God's got to offer."

I didn't really know too much about Christianity and as most of the Christians I knew had been in the faith for quite a few years I took them as role models. They were my mentors really. I adopted their values and hung on to the things they said. I used to go to endless meetings, twice to church every Sunday, never missed. Home group during the week, conferences and seminars on this and that.

I was praying lots and doing lots of things but nothing much was really happening. I didn't seem to be able to get started somehow. So I embarked on a number of things because I figured it's something that I'm not doing, something I've got to find, something I've got to do that's going to release this key. Unfortunately, each thing that I tried made me feel more rejected by the Lord.

My wife and I tried a lot of things along the way, over the years. We went into Christian fostering and praise and worship seminars. I became a Sunday school teacher and all sorts of things. Each thing left me feeling a little bit more empty. I just couldn't work it out.

Then, about six years ago, I thought, "Yep, I know what it is. I know what it is that's going to see this release of God in my life. A wilderness experience, that's what I need."

So I packed up my bags, took three days off, and headed up into the mountains. I just sat around in a cabin up there and after two days I was feeling so lonely and so lousy it was turning into a really horrible experience. God didn't say anything. I was crying out and fasting and he didn't say anything to me and it really started to leave serious doubts in me about my faith. When I got home I started to question whether this was real. Yet deep down inside I knew God was real, he'd touched me those years before, but I just couldn't get a handle on this Christianity. Everything I tried just didn't work.

Eventually, I started to give up. I just couldn't be bothered and I couldn't see the point of struggling anymore. It just didn't seem real.

Well believe it or not, God is really faithful. I'd had a friend from my youth, and we had a really open and honest relationship. When we got together there was nothing much we couldn't talk about. It was a special relationship. Last year he contacted me. I hadn't heard from him for about five years or so and we started to get back in touch again. I noticed through the letters and phone calls that there was something different about him. I knew something had happened and it made me really curious. Eventually, he came and visited me and just like when we were young, we headed off hiking for the weekend and to have a good talk. I asked him about what had happened but he didn't really say very much about it. As I talked to him I could see that he had something there that I didn't have. I was really curious about what had happened but he couldn't give it to me in a sentence.

I started to unload on him. I started to tell him about all the disappointments and the discouragement and the pain that I was feeling inside. I told him about how sinful I was and what was happening in my life. How God had forgotten me because I wasn't righteous enough. I just opened the doors and let it all out.

His response really floored me. He just accepted me. Not a word of condemnation. It just blew me right away.

I started to get a bit annoyed with God. I thought, "You've given him something. How come you haven't given that to me?" Then it started to dawn on me that my friend knew and was secure in the fact that God accepted him just like he was, warts and all. He wasn't trying to perform. I started to think, "Does God really accept me? I've tried all these things and they didn't work. Perhaps he just accepts me anyway?"

I thought I had God's economy all sorted out, God's value system. I started to realize I wasn't going to earn God's approval through my performance. I don't have to be at a certain level of righteousness for him to accept me. It was a hard lesson to learn and it took a lot of years.

– Male carpenter aged 41

Working to repay your soul affair or working to feel more spiritually safe is not limited to those within a church culture. In the so-called New Age movement, the unstated premise is that if you follow this course, try this method, listen to this guru, find your "special" teacher, and do enough work on your self, then you will eventually find happiness. Activity may produce feelings of security, but this path is the opposite end of the spectrum to true spiritual freedom. Absolute spiritual release comes to those who can embrace total powerlessness, while at the same time feel no fear. Buddhists call this enlightenment; Christians call it dying to self.

The attempt to achieve spiritual security through our own efforts may explain, in part, a strange anomaly that appeared in the British survey. Almost half (46%) of churchgoers said they had never experienced God or a presence or power. Perhaps church for many of these people is not about connecting with the divine, but rather about participating in religious procedures which make them feel spiritually safe and secure. It would also explain why some congregants and theological experts are hostile towards unorthodox soul affairs.

When I was 14, I had what I call a "moment of clarity." I was walking up a path with no clear direction in mind when I noticed/became aware that each of my steps, for about 20 feet, was absolutely pristine and clear. I'd never felt such a purity of mind and clarity of surroundings before, and never to that extent again. I can't really explain it.

That experience really changed my life. From then on I began to ask questions about our existence, God, and what we're doing here – our purpose. I pursued more spiritual topics, whereas before I'd been quite disinterested in such things.

Many years later, I was at a social function and I fell into a conversation with a Catholic theologian. I talked to him about my experiences. He became quite aggressive in his manner and words towards me. I mentioned "enlightenment" and being "fulfilled," but he said that was too intangible. He said he only believed in the written word, church doctrine, and holy scripture, what you can touch and read. He refused to believe that I could get "enlightened." No matter how much I explained it, enlightenment was a concept he refused to accept. He reckoned I had experienced God, as he knew it. He was hostile and belligerent the whole time. He refused to accept the realities of my experience, saying it was too intangible.

Before this conversation I thought everyone kept their options open and would accept stories of such experiences with an open mind. But stuff like this that shatters their beliefs scares people and they have a strong reaction to it.

It was my first experience of how really ignorant some people are.

– Male technician aged 32

We fear that which we cannot control. Soul affairs, being random and spontaneous, remain beyond individual and institutional control. Instinctively, people, like the theologian, who perceive such reports as threatening the established order, reject whatever doesn't fit into their safe, familiar framework. It's common, then, for those who venture to discuss their soul affair with religious professionals, to find themselves brushed off, their experience discounted or subjected to scrutiny.

The deeply entrenched need to control is one of the main reasons why Western religious institutions, supposedly the earthly facilitators between humans and the divine, have been so deafeningly silent or openly hostile to the overwhelming evidence of God or a presence or higher power entering the lives of ordinary people.

CHAPTER ELEVEN

SOUL AFFAIRS AND WESTERN RELIGION

[Religion] has two faces: one the face of truth, the other the face of deception

– Arthur Schopenhauer[1]

I must confess I am extremely uncomfortable writing about "the church" for I am no expert. I have no theological qualifications, have never held a paid position in any religious organization, nor undertaken any course of religious study. Nevertheless, I write because a voice from the laity and the voices of others from the secular world are seldom heard. I also suspect that many in the church do not take ordinary people's experiences of a presence or power or God seriously. One of the main reasons for this – power and control – was discussed in the previous chapter. Indeed, one prominent Christian researcher I spoke to dismissed the findings of the Oxford Religious Experience Unit as "mere coincidences." Others, too, have had their experience discounted by religious professionals.

—◉—

In the early 1970s, I accompanied a tour of the Holy Land, which was led by an Anglican Dean of the city I was currently living in. I wasn't particularly religious although I had been brought up in the Church of England.

I was sent by the company I worked for (I was PR manager) who had organized the tour through its travel department. I was included as a bit of moral support for the Dean. The rest of the tour was excessively aged women – "the lame and the game" I called them.

We visited many of the key places Christ had been. I particularly remember the spot near Capernaum, overlooking the Sea of Galilee, where Christ delivered the Sermon on the Mount.

It was a beautiful, sunny spring day and the Dean read aloud from the Bible the words that Christ spoke. I don't know if it was the heady atmosphere of being in a place with so much history attached to it, but as he read something just clicked inside me. Suddenly, everything that Christ stood for made complete sense. It was a sort of revelation, just like the last piece of a Rubik's cube falling into place. It all became simple and clear.

Later, I discussed with the Dean the question of the simplicity, as I saw it, of Christ's message and life. We had a strong exchange over this. He claimed that Christ was a more complicated proposition and required years of study before he could be fully understood. I guess if you're a member of the priesthood you need to do this sort of thing to keep the lay rabble in check. If I could get it this simply and quickly, it might mean all his study was redundant.

Any "priesthood" in any industry always has a complicated view of things; they have to really, otherwise how else can they justify their position? I heard somewhere that when some IBM technicians looked at the first Apple computer, they said it would never survive because it was too simple to operate! I think the church is similar to that. They have a workshop manual on one knee trying to run things, whereas what I had revealed to me that day had such a profound, beautiful, and natural simplicity, you couldn't doubt it.

My experience at Capernaum hasn't changed my life. I haven't become super religious, but it has given me a quiet certainty that Christ was right. For me, it was the day the penny dropped.

I've talked to hardly anyone about this, partly because I don't really want to give the scoffers another chance to scoff, but mainly because it is a personal experience which I still find difficult to communicate fully.

— Man aged 28 at the time of the experience

Unlike professional theologians and clergy, people who work and live routine lives have little knowledge of things divine apart from their own experience. This being the case, when they attempt to make sense of their sacred experiences the authoritative access point for information is Western religion's shopfront window, the church. Whatever else one might say about the church, its clergy generally do have a considerable body of expertise on spiritual matters and this cannot be dismissed. For this reason alone it is the place many of us will go to make sense of our soul affairs, to look for answers to life's big questions. However, the journey of an ecclesiastical consumer is a long one and far from easy.

I was in my 30s when a series of personal crises in my work and family life began to pose too many questions that had no answer in the secular world. Why are we here? How do we ensure justice? What is the secret to finding peace and contentment? Who is God? How does God work? It wasn't so much a question of God's existence, but of how to connect. What part of God was me? What part of me was God? The angst finally became too much and it triggered a response. After more than a decade and a half of self-imposed exile, I set out to find some answers through the church.

At this stage of my life, I was living near a small rural Catholic community. Many of my friends were members and I enjoyed hanging out with them on the weekends, attending functions, and occasionally helping with the farm activities. My wife and children were very involved, as were my friends' families. I liked the community's quiet, practical way of living out their faith. There was no proselytizing, no hard sell, no gauche outpouring of embarrassing emotions. They had a very healthy view of "mother church," being able to embrace her excesses and foibles, ignoring those rules that seemed petty or irrelevant, yet still remaining part of her and acknowledging her authority. I felt very comfortable in this environment. But because I wasn't Catholic by birth I felt I couldn't belong, that unless I converted I would always be an illegitimate outsider. So I decided to try a Protestant church to see if it might provide some answers.

One Sunday morning, I found myself in a small Pentecostal church. I was repelled by the desperation and tone of the congregation and preaching, but deeply moved by the music. I found tears running down my face. I couldn't stop them. What was happening? Something had been triggered deep inside. I went a couple more Sundays. The preacher even paid me a visit. He was a nice enough man, but when it came to exchanging ideas we may as well have been talking different languages. His frequent use of fundamentalist clichés sounded awkward and odd to me. I couldn't relate to it. I also discovered that the social-justice Christ I talked about certainly wasn't the Jesus he knew. I'm sure he was as puzzled with me as I was with him.

Soon afterwards we left New Zealand and moved to a new city in Australia. A few months after settling in, I noticed that the local Uniting church had a large number of cars parked outside on Sunday evenings. I went one night and discovered why. The minister preached for a carefully prepared and well-researched seven minutes. It was inspiring stuff. He was the first cleric I'd ever heard who I could relate to. He was honest. He spoke frankly about his own doubts and struggles with faith. In a personal conversation, I once asked him what his biggest fear was and he candidly replied, "That there is no God." It was my first experience of someone in the priesthood who saw doubt not as a sin but as a starting point to explore faith.

Inspired by his authenticity, I started attending a midweek study group. It was to be the first of many such groups as I moved to new cities and suburbs over the next few years. They were not easy places for me. Some people were so reluctant to talk about God that I couldn't understand why they even turned up. Unless there was a particularly enlightened group leader, scripture study would often turn into an academic comprehension exercise. There were very few occasions when people spoke openly from their hearts. When someone did, it was often followed by an awkward silence. Openness, transparency, and doubt were not safe attitudes to exhibit in this environment. Unorthodox personal encounters with God were also treated with circumspection and embarrassment.

Yet for a few years, I was fortunate enough to be in a couple of small groups that were wonderfully open, caring, and frank. The litmus test of these groups was that my wife, who doesn't "do God," could comfortably take part in them. These groups nurtured me. So did my reading of religious authors such as Anthony de Mello and Henri Nouwen who, rather than offering dogma and explanations of God, sought to help their readers explore their own connection points with the divine.

Because of my filmmaking career I have traveled extensively. On my trips I used to sample churches. Different countries, different cities, different neighborhoods, I would go to whichever church was nearest: Catholic, Anglican, United, Baptist, Quaker, Methodist – it didn't matter. What I was after didn't depend on any particular denomination. I was looking for an authentic interface between humans and God and I thought church was the place to find this. To my surprise and frustration, I found it extremely hard to find other people who were there for the same reason.

In my experience both at home and overseas, sermons seemed to be logical expositions presenting scripture-based arguments to explain why we should believe and have faith. Some were "feel good" psychology lectures, which, like a Chinese dinner, filled me up at the time, but left me hungry again a few hours later. Many clerics went out of their way to say nothing that might offend the congregants and consequently ended up with such sanitized spiels that there was little I could understand let alone relate to. They were extremely boring, bad lectures. Even those sermons that were well-executed failed to satisfy.

As ironic as it seems, many churches simply lacked soul. I later discovered I was not alone in feeling this. Author William Hendricks conducted "exit polls" of people in the United States who were leaving the church. He discovered that often they had gone to church looking for God but gave up when they didn't find God there.

I once talked about preaching with a friend of mine who was a great preacher. People came back week after week to hear his messages, which was ironic because he was not what I would call an outstanding communicator. Neither would he. But no one found him boring, and his sermons produced noticeable changes in people's lives.

I asked him what he thought a preacher's objective should be. I assumed he would say something about teaching and instruction, as his sermons were known for that. But he surprised me with something very unexpected: "I think the point of the sermon is to help people meet God, to have an encounter with God. Somewhere during that message, I want every person to have the experience of hearing God saying something to him or her personally. I'm not even that interested in what happens later, after they leave. As long as they meet God in that moment."

It was a novel approach, and I was reminded of it as my interviewees described their experiences with sermons. They were bored, but not necessarily because the preachers they had heard were boring communicators. Some were rather brilliant. No, they were bored spiritually; they had no experience of God. The church service was just another meeting, the sermon just another harangue, no matter how well delivered.[2]

Many sermons I heard hardly mentioned God at all. Divine intervention in our everyday lives was as absent a topic in the pulpit as it was in the secular world. This is not to say the congregants and clergy weren't well meaning, charitable people. Many were exemplary citizens and fine human beings, but the church culture more often than not ensured that authentic experiences of God – soul affairs – were seldom on the agenda.

When I was 19, I really got "into" Christianity. Sometimes during prayer, I felt God would talk to me. I would ask a question and sometimes an answer would come. The voice was similar to my own, but devoid of emotion, deeper, and always calming and ringing true.

Since having dropped Christianity, I have taken up insight meditation, which I find similar to prayer, but better. It is calming and introspective, but I also get a very similar "voice."

When I prayed, I'd ask specific questions and I'd get answers. I didn't know what it was that was answering me, but I know that I couldn't have come up with those answers myself. Also, when I prayed it was more "God-like" I suppose, more profound, whereas in meditation I sometimes have a clear flash of insight of "me." It's the same voice, but when I meditate it feels more like me. Up until recently, I would've said that God was in me, but now I think of God as a symbol, as something that describes otherness.

The funny thing was that even in church I found it difficult to tell people that I heard God speak. The church I attended somehow had the idea that only 1% of people ever hear God speak, so when I talked about it they looked at me as if I was mad. I think the churches are paranoid about losing power, and hearing directly from God threatens their power because it cuts right across their rituals and dogma.

– Man aged 26

In my experience, even in the Pentecostal charismatic churches, a group that topped the scales in reporting experiences of a presence or power (over 80% in some cases), the climate was not always conducive to sharing authentic experiences of God. In these churches, I heard many heartfelt testimonies of dramatic life turns through soul affairs, but they were mostly "success stories." Reports of struggle, hardship, and suffering were notably absent. The inference was that if you suffered or were not "doing well," it was because you lacked faith, weren't praying enough, weren't righteous enough, and so had fallen out of favor with God. It was these things that stopped your blessings. "Good" Christians would be rewarded, and handsomely.

I suspect that this way of thinking explained why I came across many who pretended to be full of joy and blessings, when patently they weren't. Transparent honest accounts of doubt and longing were not acceptable. Undoubtedly the soul affairs of such church groups are as real as anyone else's, but the subtle pressure to appear in a constant state of euphoria counts against their long-term authenticity.

Back home after much searching, inquiring, and "church shopping," I finally found a couple of open-hearted churches where a healthy balance existed between the doctrinal and mystical wings. Here I joined with other pilgrims who sat comfortably with the notion that faith might be an evolving process, and that doubt, myth, suffering, mystery, and soul affairs were an important part of this process.

I offer these personal details to place in context my frustration with the English-speaking church's apparent disinterest in private spiritual experiences. In so many of the churches I attended, logic seemed to be the starting point of faith. Since I had my starting point for faith in the emotional responses I felt during my soul affairs, I was always out of step.

In my conversations about soul affairs with numerous religious professionals – ordained clergy, priests, and religious scholars – when I mentioned "experiences of God" many were quite disinterested and tried to brush me off. Some assumed that I was trying to claim some personal divine favoritism, that I was looking for something that would set me apart, something that would put me in a position whereby I could set myself up as some sort of spiritual expert, perhaps even form a cult. I can't blame them for reacting this way as their theological training has no doubt taught them that God's intervention in ordinary human lives happens much less often than actually appears to be the case. From their responses it was apparent they thought my inquiries unworthy of serious consideration. Even if such soul affairs were true and even if they were occurring in the numbers I suggested, they were obviously of little religious significance, otherwise they would have heard of them. One very senior Anglican spokesman apologetically confessed to being at a complete loss to answer my questions, having no knowledge whatsoever of the topic.

One would assume that those in leadership positions in the English-speaking Western churches would be excited to hear that God is intimately involved in so many lives. (Many respondents are comfortable that it is the Judeo/Christian God they have experienced.) Why are they so guarded? So skeptical? Isn't this the revival so many churches have been earnestly working and praying for? Isn't this what evangelism's all about – that all would come to know and enjoy God? Has the need to maintain control become so pervasive that it is blocking truth? Why did so few know about the work of the Oxford Religious Experience Unit? I would have thought the church would be absolutely delighted with such evidence, seized upon the results and shouted them from the rooftops. Why the silence? I didn't get it. I still don't.

However, from my reading I have pieced together an explanation of sorts that may throw some light on how we have arrived at this state of affairs. It starts right back at the very beginnings of Christianity.

Up until the fifth century, a loosely knit group of contemplative Christian hermits and mystics existed near the river Nile in Egypt. Known as the Desert Fathers, their writings and reputation exerted a powerful influence on early Christian theology and thinking. A spiritual master supervised some, but many answered to no human authority. This meant that what they thought, wrote, and said was not subject to any checks, balances, or vetting by the church hierarchy. However, all this began to change when the first collective monastery was established in the fourth century.

In contrast to hermits, monks in monasteries were subject to rigorous orders, a burying of their individualism for the good of the community. Early in the sixth century, when St. Benedict's strict rule was introduced to all Latin-speaking monasteries except those in Ireland, the Western church moved further from the individual hermitic tradition. With the new rule, oriental asceticism was expunged and total obedience to monastic law and order was required. The die was cast for legalism to overshadow mysticism in the West.

The preference in Latin-speaking monasteries was to study scripture using the classical Greek methods of logic and argument. The mystical and experiential sides of Christianity were displaced. Truth and God were to be pursued through rigorous intellectual discipline. Emotion, the enemy of intellect, was to be avoided, for emotion obscured truth. Only facts and intellectual thoroughness could lead one to truth. These assumptions formed the basis for the way Western ideas and education were shaped ever after. They are still our cultural predisposition today.

The Eastern church by contrast didn't go down the collective monastic road. It carried on the hermitical tradition and to this day has no orders of monks. Compared to its Western counterpart, it has always been far less concerned with religious legalism. The Eastern church tended to view monasteries as an impediment to solitude and contemplation, so its branch of Christianity developed a form of solitary life. Hermits lived out of sight of each other, but close enough to join in communal devotions. One of the more famous collections of these solitaries was established in the tenth century on the holy mountain of Athos, in northern Greece. From there, solitaries were introduced to Russia where they evolved to become the highly influential *startsy* – holy wise men who lived on the edge of communities and whose counsel, advice, and spiritual guidance was sought by both rich and poor.

Compared to the reflective hermitical basis of Eastern and Celtic Christianity, our Western religious culture over the last millennium and a half has been one of suppression of the individual to the whole, be it mother church, mother monastery, or mother doctrine. Up until 1965, the Roman Catholic Church claimed it had a monopoly on absolute truth and emphasized that communication with God was primarily achieved through the church and its sacraments. Protestantism, too, carried similarly tight controls and was highly suspicious of the independent outsider. Five centuries ago, Martin Luther claimed you did not need the church in order to interact with God. But there was a catch. Protestant doctrine maintained that humans must still do something to reach God: express the conviction that Christ is God, and read and interpret scripture. Neither Catholicism nor Protestantism (with the exception of Quakerism) recognized or accepted that interaction between God and humans was by itself enough.

It seemed to be enough for the Desert Fathers, however, and it seems to be sufficient for most contemporary Westerners who choose to stay outside the church.

The cultural disposition of authorities in the Western church, both Protestant and Catholic, for order and control, has meant that historically those it considered a threat to orderliness, and especially those who thought they had some direct connection to God through a soul affair or personal prayer, have been given a rather rough time of it. Indeed, so strict has this religious legalism been that unorthodox ways of worshipping or seeking communion with God were often viewed as heresy and were destined to receive harsh and punitive treatment.

In the 14th century, the Carthusians were especially vigilant in seeking out and burning heretics – those who claimed direct experience of God. Joan of Arc (c. 1412–1431) heard celestial voices and saw visions. Although her claims were judged by a panel of French theologians to be spiritually legitimate, she was later tried and condemned for heresy for believing she was directly responsible to God rather than to the church. Twenty-five years after her death, the church retried her case, and she was pronounced innocent. In 1920, she was canonized by Pope Benedict XV. Many a great Christian saint has been a heretic and a martyr in their day – it seems to go with the territory.

St. John of the Cross (1542–1591) was bitterly persecuted by the Carmelite authorities for his support of St. Teresa's call to the mystical, meditative life, and a continual seeking of God. In 1577, his brother monks kidnapped him and kept him imprisoned in the Toledo monastery. Daily he had to suffer "circular discipline" whereby he knelt on the floor while monks walked around him lashing his bare back with leather whips. This "discipline" was later restricted to Fridays, but he was lashed with such zeal that his shoulders were crippled for life. St. Teresa even wrote to the church authorities asking that St. John be handed over to the Moors, for they at least would show more pity. He was imprisoned in a cupboard too small for him to stand up or lie down in. One night the Prior of the convent entered his cell, berated him for seeking reform, and proceeded to brutally kick him. He endured this sort of treatment for eight months, at which point, despite being physically exhausted by his imprisonment and harsh treatment, he made a dramatic escape and was given asylum in a convent of Barefoot Carmelites.[3]

Throughout Western religious history repression has often been the response to those who choose to interact directly with God rather than go through the church and her sacraments. We know from Spanish church records that in the late 15th and early 16th centuries there was a group of lay people who stressed contemplative prayer and who sought God directly. Known as *alumbrados* or "the enlightened" they didn't openly challenge the church or its sacraments but quietly sidestepped them. Rather than participate in vocal prayers, they preferred to meditate in silence and await divine illumination. Doubtless they would have had many soul affairs. In the 1520s, the Inquisition savagely suppressed such groups for being potential "Lutherans." More likely these were folk whose direct experience of God was not translatable into religious orthodoxy. Probably they were simple and uncomplicated mystics – a branch of the church which still exists.[4]

Towards the end of the 17th century a Spanish priest named Miguel de Molinos published the *Spiritual Guide*, which encouraged a style of passive meditation called quietism. This work enjoyed enormous success in Italy and was appreciated by the Quakers who saw it as promoting teachings similar to their own. Not surprisingly, the *Spiritual Guide* was denounced by the Inquisition and was banned by Rome, as it was considered such hidden practices, whereby God conducts secret conversations with individual souls via the still small voice, could undermine the authority of the church. It is only in recent times that the book has been allowed to be republished.[5]

The mystical disposition of transcendent soul affairs threatens to undermine religious authority, which is why those in positions of religious power view them with such deep suspicion. Western Christian mystics in particular have had to walk a fine line in their "union with God" lest they be seen to suggest their union places them on a par with Christ or God, or that they are gaining divine access directly rather than through the auspices of the church. Meister Eckhart (13th century) stressed the unity of God and the ability of the individual soul to become one with God during life. He said the human soul was superior to the angels and he spoke of passing beyond God to a "simple ground," a "still desert" without any distinctions, out of which all things were created – an idea very similar to that of the Tao of Lao Tzu (fifth century BCE).[6] For this and for other such unifying statements he fell out of favor with the church, his heretical status only being lifted in the 20th century.

The Western church's history of stifling soul affairs explains why I had so much trouble finding much enthusiasm or interest in the topic from Western religious officials. After so many centuries of repression, it is simply no longer on their agenda. The church's cultural predisposition to logic and argument also explains why something as emotional and spontaneous as a soul affair is not only treated with suspicion by those in positions of power, but is also a reason why churchgoers have learned to be publicly cautious of soul affairs. A church culture of disbelief now exists around the possibility that God may be actively and extraordinarily involved in the lives of the nonchurched and to any great degree among congregants. Such a culture ensures those who don't fit in move on, leaving a conservative, compliant core who will not easily accept that the reality of God and how God works might be very different from what they believe.

A couple of years ago, I had a wonderful "epiphany," I think you call it. I was walking along the cliffs overlooking the sea. I stopped for a while and just watched. The seagulls soaring, the waves breaking, the beautiful sky off to the horizon – everything just seemed to burst with creation. I could see God in everything that was there; the creation and God were just so intertwined. I find it difficult to explain. I wept at the wonder of experiencing this creation. There are few people I would tell about it who I think would understand.

The following week I shared this moment with my Bible study group, saying how intensely I experienced God in that place and in that moment. The reaction I got surprised me. One man told me I shouldn't have to go to that place to experience God, that God is all around me and I should be experiencing God all the time, especially at church. I said I found God in creation more often than in church or in scripture even. Then a woman chipped in saying I was worshipping creation not God.

I think that because my experience wasn't based on scripture or church it was somehow seen as less legitimate by them, which meant they could dismiss what I was saying. I was hurt because I was sharing something from my heart. I think when we do that we like to be heard. I expected them to ask questions and to be interested in my experience. Not to dismiss it.

I felt sorry for them really. They were missing out. It was almost as if they'd created a certain image of God, what he was and where he could be found, and what I was saying challenged that image, so perhaps they felt they had to defend it.

I experience God through creation, whether it be nature, fishermen getting a good haul of mackerel in their nets, or a Downs syndrome child playing with a dog and a ball. All of them are so completely focussed on what they're doing; they have no judgment about the right or wrongs of their situation; they are just so totally involved in the moment. It's so perfect.

I don't expect people to understand me but that doesn't matter because I think God understands me.

– Man aged 49

A reaction such as this man encountered in his study group is the culmination of legalism and organizational restrictions erecting barriers to the open acknowledgment of soul affairs. Responses such as these may also explain in part why people in the English-speaking world (with the exception of those in the United States) have largely stopped attending church on a regular basis.

In the 20 years since the first national opinion poll on religious experience was taken in 1976, British churches have lost over 2 million members and 5,000 clergy. Almost 2,000 church buildings have closed and weekly church attendance has dropped to between 3% to 5% of the population.[7] In Australia, 13% say they go every week, but surveys of attenders show only 10% actually turn up.[8] The Canadian figure of 23% of the population who say they attend church each week also needs to be viewed with caution as a study in Vancouver showed that although 18% of the city's population claimed they went, only 7% actually put in an appearance in the pews.[9] Canadian sociologist Reginald Bibby suggests one of the main reasons people no longer bother going is that churches don't deliver what their customer base is seeking – God.

Although the overall picture may be gloomy, there are still many individual churchgoers and clergy who will be extremely receptive, even delighted to hear about a personal experience of contact with God or a presence or higher power. These individuals can see past the structures and legalism and can set aside preconceptions to celebrate the sacred experiences of others. One young man was told by his parish priest that he was indeed blessed to have had an experience of God. Another woman struck a particularly intuitive member of the clergy early on in her life.

I am 55 and my experience happened when I was 17, but I remember it with great clarity. My family was all very anti-church, but I had always felt a hankering for God and an interest in religion and I was going fairly regularly to the Methodist church near my home. However, I did not really believe in the incarnation, resurrection, etc. and I never felt anyone was "out there" when I tried to pray.

One Sunday evening, I was particularly struck by something the minister said in his sermon. I remember him well: a young married man, thoughtful and sincere, not a fundamentalist or hell-fire preacher. After the service, I started asking him questions and arguing with him. A few people were standing around listening, but it got late and they drifted off. We must have talked for about an hour, and he said we would have to go. He had to lock the main door, put out the lights, and then leave by the side door, so he opened the side door to get some light from the street lamp outside. As he walked back through the darkened church, I felt a strange excitement, as if something of great portent was about to happen.

The minister was going, but I felt something had to be resolved then and there so, trying to get him to stay, I asked, "Can you feel God in this place?" He must have recognized something urgent in my voice because he came back and asked, "Would you like to pray about it?" He knelt at the communion rail and, feeling very awkward, I knelt beside him. He started praying out loud, extempore prayer common in Methodist practice.

Suddenly, far stronger than my emotions or embarrassment, I became aware that Christ was standing in front of me, on the other side of the communion rail. The sense of presence was so strong that I opened my eyes, expecting to see him, but when I didn't see anything, I was just as sure that he was there. When the minister stopped praying, I whispered to him that I felt that Christ was there, and he told me to pray and ask him into my heart. I did so, aloud, and as I prayed, I felt Christ merge into me.

All this took only a few moments. We walked out the side door and while I was waiting for the minister to finish locking up, I remember looking around and feeling a total oneness with the universe. It was not elation; I didn't feel in any way psyched up. Rather, I felt as if everything around me was ancient and I was part of it and was being almost crushed down into its age, while over it was a great, brooding presence. I remember looking around at the houses and the sky and the darkness and feeling a tremendous awe and an absolute certainty that God had created everything and was within it and within me. When I tried to explain this to the minister, he said something about my having taken the first step and I remember feeling puzzled because I could not imagine anything beyond this complete awareness of God.

Next morning as soon as I woke up, I remembered what had happened and felt my whole being turning with gratitude to God and I experienced a deep sense of bliss. For about three weeks, I was in an altered state of consciousness: I was deeply happy, I felt a close communion with God, and I loved praying. I even saw colors differently, more intense, and everything seemed to be vibrating with life. I had a great desire to pass on my wonderful new certainty, but my family was dismayed. My father said I'd "seen the light" and had become a fanatic while my mother thought I had fallen in love with someone at church. When a couple of her friends said that I looked radiant and obviously had a boyfriend, she began trying to hide it! While there was no human love interest in my life at that time, when I *did* fall madly in love for the first time some years later, it was similar in some ways to my spiritual experience.

One thing I read recently struck me – we have an experience like this and then spend the rest of our lives trying to explain it to ourselves! That experience was one-off in intensity, but I feel it opened me to the reality of the spiritual dimension and ever since it I have been able to seek and experience communion with God. At the present time, I attend church regularly but have not done so all my life, partly because I have moved around a lot and partly because I have had times of doubt, dryness, rejection, etc. But I feel my whole life has been signed by those five minutes when I was 17.

–Woman aged 55

It's heartening to hear of this minister's involvement in such a profound affair of the soul. My hope is that as we better document such affairs, all of us, both secular and religious, will become more aware of their existence. Currently, though, it's a vicious circle: no one talks about soul affairs, so we think we're alone and we keep them secret. Because we keep them so secret, religious professionals, clergy, and church office holders rarely hear about them and so have no benchmark of normality by which to judge them. As a result, clergy often assume that those who claim such experiences are "touched" and they dismiss them accordingly. Add to this the church's historical antipathy toward private spiritual experiences and these intimate encounters become even more closeted. Unfortunately, things aren't much better in the secular world.

CHAPTER TWELVE

LANGUAGE AND TABOO

The more one talks about their vision of God the more you should run away.

– Sufi saying[1]

When we travel overseas and encounter foreign languages and customs, it is instantly obvious that our way of speaking and behaving is different, that there is no one right way of seeing or doing things, that there is a multiplicity of behaviors and customs throughout the world. Some travelers can't cope with this and seek refuge in hotels where their familiar culture has been faithfully reproduced. Yet travel *does* broaden the mind, for even those who seek refuge would never deny diversity exists; they just don't like it. At home, the differences are less easy to spot.

Within our own culture, there are many subcultures. The culture of our workplace may be very different from that of our home, or the gym, or the particular social club we belong to. Each subculture has its own values and its own language. Each carries implicit and explicit understandings of what is and what isn't acceptable. To a great extent, all of us are institutionalized into the particular subcultures we move in. With no evidence to the contrary, we tend to assume that everyone views things pretty much the same way we do and when we encounter differences a common reaction is to see the other person as the odd one out, not ourselves.

When it comes to soul affairs, there is an almost impassable cultural barrier between two sets of people: those who speak a religious language and those who don't. Herein lies another layer of reason why our soul affairs remain secret. Although popular, privatized religion and public institutionalized religion may well describe similar things, neither side understands the other, nor do they accept that this state of affairs exists. I found this out the hard way a few days after emerging from my five weeks of mountain solitude, which I mentioned at the beginning of the book.

At a dinner party, I talked about my passionate affair of the soul with a few old friends. The experiences I related had them intrigued and they listened intently. When they'd last seen me 20 or so years before, I had not appeared in the least bit religious or spiritually inclined. At this stage, so soon after my soul affair, I was using religious terms to describe my experience, for they seemed to fit. Unfortunately, our conversation was overheard by a couple of strangers, who found what I was saying confronting and who began to argue. They were soon joined by a few more strangers, who assumed I was some sort of religious fundamentalist and, sensing open season, waded in. It seemed the words I was using were striking some incredibly raw nerves. Some mocked me, some patronized me, one was extremely vicious in his verbal attack. I ended up in a long and particularly heated argument with one woman. It was most unpleasant.

The whole episode left me feeling ashamed and sullied. In being drawn into their conversation and opening myself up to a cynical group of strangers, I'd cheapened one of the most important moments of my life. I felt I'd betrayed a part of me that was most precious. I was angry with myself for being such a fool, for allowing myself to get caught in a position where my deepest spiritual intimacies were on show. It took me a long time to recover from this bruising verbal brawl. I was terribly wounded.

But I was also intrigued. Why did my revelation of a soul affair provoke such condemnation and reproach from strangers, but not from my old friends? Why acceptance from them and criticism from the others? It took me a long time and much thought to work out what had happened.

At first I thought I had given offense by discussing religion, but I rejected that explanation as religious beliefs, especially those of Buddhism, Hinduism, Taoism, and Confucianism are openly accepted and tolerated. Indeed, there is an active intellectual curiosity displayed towards non-Western religions. However, a claimed encounter with "God" is a completely different matter. When such an encounter is described using religious language, the reaction can be openly hostile. I had made the disastrous mistake of using the wrong language in the wrong place at the wrong time. It's not as if I didn't know the rules.

Through my film work, I have been made vitally aware of how I can be accepted or dismissed based on the language I use. In filming documentary and TV information programs I regularly move between many different worlds. Within the space of a few hours, I can go from dealing with destitute homeless people to top-level bank managers, from being with the heads of state one week to filming barely literate farm workers the next. I never know what to expect. But I *do* know how important it is to use the right language in order to gain entrance to the various worlds I visit. I even made a film about this once. It was a fascinating exercise and I learned a lot.

The film's chief content adviser was a senior linguist from a local university who suffered from chronic fatigue syndrome (ME). This was back in the days before ME had been given official medical recognition and the common assumption was that those who claimed to suffer from ME were malingering. This was supposition on the part of the medical fraternity as no detailed research into ME had ever been undertaken.

Fed up with having her illness dismissed as a psychosomatic complaint, our content adviser/linguist set about lobbying for appropriate medical research to be undertaken to determine whether or not ME had a biological origin. Being a good academic, she thoroughly researched the topic and submitted a document outlining what she thought was an excellent case to the State Department of Health and asking for research funds. It was rejected.

Undeterred she applied again, this time with even more medical information from experts. This submission was also rejected. Frustrated, she asked to see examples of previous successful submissions. These she linguistically analyzed and from them extracted the "language of medical research funding submissions." She then rewrote her submission using this language. Presto! Her submission was not only accepted, but given priority! When asked to present her case before a panel of experts, they were amazed that she wasn't a medical researcher – the submission was couched in such terms that they believed only a highly qualified doctor could have been the author. The funding was granted, the research was undertaken, and a sound medical basis for ME was uncovered.

The linguist realized that if there was a specific language for medical research and Health Department submissions, then within groups of other professionals such as lawyers, social scientists, physicists, economists, and historians as well as plumbers, computer technicians, marketers, and mechanics – in fact within all groups – specific language patterns would also exist. By analyzing such patterns, she cracked the codes to effective communication within the groups. In so doing, she saw that here was a great opportunity to demystify for school students, the codes associated with different subjects. If she could teach them how to write in the language of a particular discipline, they, like she, would be in a much better position to succeed. Based on this key concept, new teaching programs were initiated. Now, schools help their students identify the language rules peculiar to each subject area. This genre-based teaching method has proven to be especially helpful to students for whom English is a second language. What was once confusing is now clear. Prior to teaching this methodology it tended to be only the brighter students who intuitively picked up the subtle differences between language styles.

I found all this quite a revelation. I had never been particularly good in science at school and thought it was because I lacked aptitude. This may well have been the case, but it didn't help that I read science textbooks in the same way I read novels, skipping the boring bits and looking for the plot! It explained, perhaps, why my classmates who excelled at science found English tedious. By reading novels slowly and literally, they missed nuances and subtexts. Fascinating!

When I applied this linguistic rationale to the language of soul affairs, it became obvious why I received such an abrasive reaction at the dinner party. Like the medical panel, the strangers rejected that which was culturally unfamiliar to them. I may well have been talking about something that they had also experienced, but unless I expressed it in their language they would be hard pressed to recognize the similarities. What they heard was someone using the "language of Western religion," and in their experience people who used such language were offensive proselytizers doing a religious hard or soft sell.

Canadian sociologist Reginald Bibby notes that a history of religious hucksterism brought about by televangelism and dubious sales techniques "is a particular expression of faith repugnant to all but a few adherents. Unfortunately, there are enough individuals to reinforce this snake oil mentality to give the illusion that this is what Christianity is all about."[2] This con artist reputation meant that no matter what I said, the strangers wouldn't have heard it. All they could hear was the ugly agenda of a religious sales pitch.

When I look back at that time at the dinner party, I am now horrified at what transpired, for in the strangers' eyes I was a proselytizing evangelist. No wonder I provoked such a harsh reaction. My friends, on the other hand, knew me well enough to be bemused rather than offended by what I was saying. Interestingly, I faced another hostile reaction a few months later, this time from the other side.

I was at a Christian study group meeting. I had been attending for a few months and on this particular evening I talked about some of my spiritual ideas using secular language, for now, thanks in part to the dinner party, I was at pains to express myself using as religiously neutral language as I could. However, the language I used pushed a button for one woman who assumed I was some sort of New Ager and who took it upon herself to put me straight. After the meeting broke up, we had a very strong discussion for about 20 minutes on the front lawn. Because I hadn't used Christian rhetoric, she was convinced my opinion was not legitimate. I particularly remember her trying to convince me that there was an evil presence in the world. I concurred with her over and over again, but she couldn't hear it. She kept coming back at me with different examples to prove her case, because in her experience people who used religiously neutral language wouldn't hold her point of view.

The languages of the secular and religious worlds are so alien to each other that the same words can trigger totally opposite reactions. The words "Holy Spirit," "The Lord," and "Satan," may be comfortable to churchgoers but will be offensive in most secular circles. In fact, I can think of few other words so guaranteed to stop all conversation dead and have people heading for "elsewhere" as fast as they can. As the saying goes, the quickest way to stop a conversation at a party is to mention the words "Jesus Christ" – unless of course you're swearing! The languages of the secular and religious worlds are irreconcilably polarized. That there is so little common ground between these two extremes is due to a potent mix of uncontrolled fundamentalism, science, and silence.

The theological debates that raged throughout the late 19th and early 20th centuries triggered a set of events that ostensibly killed mainstream society's belief in God. Darwin's theory of evolution; the scientific method which emphasizes repeatable, measurable proofs; Engels' and Marx's contention that religion is the opiate of the masses; Freud's psychoanalytical contention that belief in God represents a childhood desire to be looked after by a father figure; and, more recently, economic rationalism; all combined to drive God off the thinking person's intellectual agenda. Given such an overwhelming body of evidence, only fools, the emotionally unstable or mentally unhinged would continue to believe in such a childish concept as a divine omnipotent being. To publicly admit belief in a supernatural higher power or in any spiritual form of otherness, let alone to claim you'd had an experience of it, became open invitation to mockery.

With physical and social science landing body blows to faith, public belief in God became increasingly isolated. Partitioned off from the mainstream, Christianity became a religious island in a secular sea – a place where people went for an hour or so each week, and spoke an esoteric language. Churchgoers became shy and embarrassed by their faith activities. Faith was now seen as peculiar or quaint, something even to be ashamed of. Private belief became so removed from any social context that it went totally underground, relegated to lie alongside other personal deep dark secrets and our most intimate experiences. Non-belief was now accepted as the norm, especially if you were educated.

Yet privately it was, *and still is*, another story.

Recent figures show that, on average, more than four-fifths of Westerners believe in God. Almost 50% of Canadians say they have experienced God's presence,[3] 87% of Americans say they pray every day, and 63% of Australians pray at least occasionally.[4] Of the 41% of Americans who have no church connection, George Gallup discovered that 45% still pray every day and 64% believe Jesus is God or the Son of God.[5] Almost two-thirds (64%) of Australians believe that there is a "God who concerns Himself with every human being personally."[6] Currently we live in the paradoxical situation of widespread private belief coexisting alongside entrenched public disbelief.

Institutionalized disbelief is given added impetus by the fact that highly respected professional groups – doctors, psychologists, and psychiatrists – tend to view religious faith as akin to superstition and unworthy of serious consideration. Indeed, so entrenched has the secularization of psychiatric medicine become that psychiatrist M. Scott Peck once felt it necessary to deliver a broadside to his colleagues for viewing religion as inferior and pathological.[7]

Peck accused his peers of being excessively secular and of consistently neglecting the issue of spirituality to the detriment of their profession and their patients. He gave the example of a woman in her 60s, who, after a lifetime of being mentally healthy, had suddenly developed an intense psychosis. After three years of expensive hospital treatment, she showed no signs of improvement and her husband asked Peck to investigate. In his first interview with this woman, Peck established that prior to the onset of her illness she'd left the Presbyterian church, where she had spent 40 years as an active member, and joined a much more liberal denomination. The fact that she had changed churches never appeared on any of her medical records. The psychiatrists currently in charge of her case were not only unaware of this event, but were also ignorant of the rest of her spiritual history. Peck's suggestions on how to address this issue, which he believed to be relevant to her psychiatric condition, were not taken up and she was later transferred to a nursing home. Because psychiatry did not take religious faith seriously it had a lopsided view of the human condition, which severely reduced the effectiveness of its therapies.

The medical profession is not the only one blinkered to spiritual matters. In most professional circles nowadays, to openly admit faith is to invite incredulity and run the risk of becoming an embarrassment to your colleagues. I can recall having many furtive discussions with my television colleagues over photocopiers, in corridors, or in quiet areas. The conversations were covert because in my industry, as in many others, overt expressions of faith in God, a presence, or power are socially unacceptable. If you express such a faith in Christian terms it will also be assumed that you are a fundamentalist.

Within a context of widespread public disbelief, fundamentalism has increasingly become the public face of Christianity. It requires strong nerves and even stronger convictions to withstand open disapproval and social exclusion. Consequently, those who *do* swim against the social tide and who are outspoken about their Christianity tend to be those who are more dogmatically driven or who are convinced that they are a divinely appointed messenger. Those who harbor doubts and who do not wish to expose their spiritual intimacies to a skeptical audience keep silent, further increasing the public perception that most Protestant Christians are fundamentalists – an impression strengthened in part by the changing nature of church attendance.

Coinciding with the growth of public disbelief has been a mass exodus from the mainstream churches. Church attendance in all Western countries except the United States is a fraction of what it was in the 1950s. This means that the proportion of Christians in the more conservative fundamentalist and "happy clappy" charismatic churches has risen dramatically. Through smart marketing and effective use of the media, such conservative branches of Christianity have constantly thrust themselves into the public domain. Although these churches encourage open expression of soul affairs, most people are temperamentally unsuited to such overt outpourings of emotionalism.

Charismatics and fundamentalists are also the ones at the grassroots level who will most readily admit to being Christian, and seize every opportunity to "witness" (proselytize) to their brand of religion. We've probably shared workplaces and lecture halls with such people, been accosted by them on the streets, found them knocking on our doors, had impassioned relatives and once close friends break every Christian principle they claim to believe in, simply to make a point. A work colleague once confided to me that he didn't like "fish people," the nickname he gave proselytizing Christians because of their fish-shaped bumper stickers. His disdain for them centered around his sister's attempts over two years to get him to convert and join her church. He'd only managed to stop her constant harassment by refusing to visit and by forbidding her to visit him. He was quite hurt and embittered by the whole affair. Another young man brought up in a liberal church environment became so fundamentalist in his thinking that he turned on his "heretical" parents and didn't speak to them for years. He abandoned his studies to work for his new church. This caused immense pain to the parents who had similar beliefs but expressed them differently.

Horror stories abound and enough of us have experienced such excesses firsthand to know their reality. The behavior of a fervent, highly visible minority has stained all Christianity with the tinge of eccentricity, so much so that these days the term "born again" or even the word "Christian" is often used as a term of derision. Although church charitable organizations and high-profile individuals such as Bishop Desmond Tutu and the late Mother Teresa have earned widespread acceptance and approval in secular circles, the word "Christian" and the institution itself have not.

The contempt displayed towards proselytizing Protestant Christians and by association all Christians, has been made worse by the silence of the more considered elements of Christianity – the Roman Catholic, Anglican, and mainstream Protestant churches. The silence of these denominations has allowed the public face of Western religion to be marginalized out to the fanatical fringe. In response to fundamentalist Christians, secular society has mentally lumped all Christians in with borderline folk who have strange beliefs. An effective and rigorous societal taboo is now in place against Christians and Christian language. The merest whiff of it will draw a quick and sudden reaction.

This is what I had struck at the dinner party. This is why many keep their soul affairs secret.

The agenda attached to Christianity has created a severe problem for those who would like to express their soul affairs using Christian terminology. One woman I spoke to had to arrange a time to phone when her husband was out, because if he heard her talking about such matters he would get angry. Our conversation was abruptly halted when he arrived home unexpectedly. So strong is this taboo that it makes even more secret what was already hidden.

To get around the prejudice against the word Christian, those who attend mainstream churches increasingly describe themselves by their denomination rather than their faith: "I am Catholic," or "I'm an Anglican," or "I go to Mass," or "I go to Springfield Uniting Church." Anything to avoid using the word of shame: "Christian."

Generally, these are more socially acceptable statements, but they still need to be treated with caution depending on the circumstances. Many people have had bad experiences of "churchianity" as children and do not wish to expose their children or themselves to such mistreatment again. Add to this the continual discovery of unchecked, institutionalized pedophilia and sexual abuses within religious organizations, and we now have thoroughly discredited institutions.

In 1980, 60% of Canadian said they had a "great deal" or "quite a bit" of confidence in religious leaders. Ten years later, after the revelations of horrific abuse and scandals, made exponentially worse by clumsy and inept damage control efforts, Canadians gave their bruised and battered religious leadership a confidence rating of only 37%.[8] Similar scandals rocked the church in Australia as it became evident that cruel despots had been allowed to run virtual slave camps of children entrusted to their care.

The stain is nowhere near removed. There are enough cases of sexual abuse by clergy, priests, and brothers trickling through the courts to convince the public that little has changed, that office holders in these institutions need to be carefully watched. Making the situation even worse is an apparently indifferent head office that has either turned a blind eye or covered up the inexcusable criminal behavior of its employees. The net result is that too many clergy have become terribly tainted. Institutions that were once trusted have become the butt of jokes. The excesses of the few have poisoned the wells. It has been an extremely serious problem for Western Christianity, both Protestant and Catholic, and the scars run deep.

Thankfully there is some light at the end of the tunnel. Pope John Paul II's public apology at the beginning of the 21st century for Catholics' "faults of the past" – including silence on slavery, oppression of women, doctrinal antipathy to Jews, and inhumanity towards those tortured and killed during the Inquisition's search for heretics – is a wonderful start to the reconciliation process.

Yet despite the taboo against and debased currency of contemporary Christianity, it is still the foundation of our culture. Christianity is the official religion of Western countries. Our national anthems and constitutions invariably contain references to the Christian God. Our ethical, legal, and moral attitudes owe much to Christianity. This being the case, those who do not consider themselves particularly religious may still express their soul affairs in traditional Christian terms.

I am a karate teacher and have studied it for 30 years. My experience occurred in early June, 1977, and it was of such power and clarity that I am unable to forget it. The situation was brought about by a general dissatisfaction with my life and where it was going, a very strong sense of being lost, and finally, what appeared to be the breakdown of my marriage.

On the particular day (a Sunday), I had finally come to a point where I felt I had no more energy or willpower to fight and resist the things that were happening in my life. I was kneeling on the floor of my friend's lounge room next to my wife. My friend and his wife were in the room and we were talking about the sadness and hopelessness of the situation. My friend, a Christian, said something about how I felt (I can't remember what) and at that moment a feeling rose from the base of my spine, right up through my body, to the crown of my head, where this rushing of "energy" seemed to be released. My whole body and my character (or mind) seemed at peace. I said, "I think I've just found myself," and then, "No, it's what people call God. It's in me."

It was the most real moment I'd ever experienced. I was getting information from my deepest parts. What I felt was – and this sounds really strange – that at a certain point, I was God. Not that I'm the big guy in the sky overlooking everything, but I felt I was "me" at my purest level, and the more "me" I became, the more God I became. I use the word God, but it is God the force, the power, the universe, everything.

My wife was stunned, even worried. I said to her, "It's all okay. Everything is just as it should be. Things are only bad if you think they are, or good if you think they are." I turned to my friend and said, "I've never felt like I am in the room before! It's always been as though there was a glass wall between me and the rest of the people in the room."

At that moment, I felt we were all experiencing the absolute moment of now. My thoughts were still being thought, but "I" was simply watching them come up. "I" was watching us talk from a different "psychic" place. It's very hard to put into words.

When we drove home I kept thinking, "This is what everyone is looking for." I told my wife that and she asked, how did I know. My answer was, "I just know. Everything just is." This made me laugh. I felt that at last I was free and I had spent all of my life thinking I wasn't free. This amused me even more and then I thought that my life was perfect; the good and the bad, the ups and the downs, all had brought me to this moment.

Driving home that night the words of the 23rd Psalm came to me and I realized, laughing, that it was all true, every bit of it.

When the words, "The Lord is my shepherd, I will not want" came to me, it meant the energy source within me is my shepherd and it cannot be extinguished; it guides me and if I tune in to it – if I let go of "me" and let myself be taken along – it's wonderful. When I saw that, I laughed, because it's all about being alive in this moment and trusting in the "force" within me.

I wouldn't say that I believe; that's far too tame. I *know!* I have to *feel* it to know it. It's why I don't like being in church – there are just a lot of rules to follow. I said to my wife, "I feel as though I have just met Jesus; I know his mind."

I slept beautifully and awoke in awe of life. The next day was wonderful. My body felt as though it flowed through the day. Everything was brighter, clearer, and more wonderful than before, even though I was seeing the same scenery and people. I wrote a poem about it and it felt like the poem wrote itself, as though the poem existed "somewhere" and I just wrote it down.

When it first happened, I "inverted" myself. In a sense, I went out of my mind. I changed in that I became much more responsible. Up until then, I thought life was just something that happened to you, whether it be good luck or bad. But I accept now that it's your attitude that counts. As the days passed, so did my state of mind. After the Wednesday, it became a memory that has dominated my life and has led me in a totally different direction. I went from no understanding of God and no interest to a point where I pray regularly to God and Jesus, and I live my life according to the words of Jesus. I haven't gone to church much because the times I've been, I've realized from the way the ministers spoke that they have never had this experience and they are talking from their minds and not their hearts. I felt as though my heart had opened up on that night in 1977, and that feeling of God was the same as that of pure love and in fact was my inner self. "The kingdom of heaven is within you" is actually true.

Nowadays, I live my life much as I always did. Things go wrong and things go right. I have wins and losses, and yet life goes on. I wish I could say that my life is now wonderful, with no worries and no doubting of God, but that isn't true. I still doubt; I still get depressed; I still have down times, laugh, and have fun; but I know that this is my life and that this is how it is meant to be. In a sense, it is perfect in its imperfection.

I've become quite "Christian," not in the sense that I go to church (which I don't), but in that I now see what Jesus Christ was on about. He wasn't talking about moral codes and rules; it's a system he wanted us to follow that allows you to get in touch with a higher power.

I think that if I'd been born in another culture, I'd probably give my experience another name and wouldn't use the Christian stuff. It's probably because I was brought up in the Church of Christ until I was 12 and I couldn't wait to get out of there.

I told around four or five close friends at the time, but over the last 25 years I wouldn't have told more that 15 people. You have to be very careful who you say it to as they think you're a bit touched.

– Man late 40s

It is these, our private spiritual experiences, our secret affairs of the soul, that feed the fires of faith. It is truly astonishing that in an era when public disbelief is so entrenched such a universal underground private spirituality appears not only to survive but to absolutely thrive. That it can flourish with no infrastructure, no memberships, and no organizational networks is remarkable. It does so simply because the reality of our soul affairs is so compelling.

Because our soul affairs are so powerful and diverse, there is a tremendous appetite for open all-inclusive explorations into spiritual matters. Due to public disbelief, such forays into the spiritual realms are an intensely personal business. Quietly, millions of us go about surreptitiously pursuing our interest in secret, lest we encounter some of the problems I've referred to above. With the public face of Christianity so discredited outside of theological circles, Western religion has largely been abandoned as a means to explore such issues. Instead, the demand is now being fed through sources that neither the theological nor the secular world would recognize as being particularly religious. It is to these areas we now turn to find the voices that give expression to the profound mysteries we've experienced through our secret affairs of the soul.

CHAPTER THIRTEEN

HOW TO EXPRESS THE INEXPRESSIBLE

Called or Not Called, God is Present.

— Carved on a stone tablet over Dr. Carl Jung's door.[1]

Over the last couple of decades, there has been a virtual explosion in the number of people searching for meaning through secular rather than religious channels. In many mainstream bookshops, as much as a third of the nonfiction section is devoted to self-awareness, self-help, and spirituality. Some retailers specialize entirely in these subjects. The appetite for credible spiritual food appears to be insatiable, and here, between the covers, we can discreetly hunt for the concepts and ideas that give expression to our private spiritual pillow talk, our deepest innermost thoughts, our secret affairs of the soul.

Books are the new, preferred medium for soul searching, for we can accept or reject the printed word without having to defend our decisions or have our opinions subjected to cynical scrutiny. Books represent a highly successful "narrow casting" medium. By contrast, the broadcast mediums of television and to a lesser extent radio, rarely discuss nonfiction spirituality as they cannot express a personalized intimate experience in the way a book can. When viewing TV in our living areas, others can see our reactions and, due to the culture of public disbelief, this makes watching such programs a potentially embarrassing exercise, regardless of whether or not we've had a soul affair. The privacy of the written word, however, circumvents public disbelief, as no one needs to know what we are reading at any particular time.

A book often becomes a special part of our private journey as we travel with it through the days or weeks we spend reading. Sometimes books act as catalysts, breaking down our preconceptions and making us more predisposed to a soul affair than might otherwise be the case.

I come from a background as a professional sportsman while also involving myself in the nightclub scene, which for me included ecstasy, speed, and girls. It was always important for me to look good – no matter how I really felt about myself – and to show myself to be extremely confident to everyone around me.

I was extremely heavily into body building and I found myself lifting larger weights than my body could handle. As a result, one day in the gym I badly pulled my trapezius (shoulder muscle). At the time, I was working with a girl who offered to pray for it after work one day.

I was actually just humoring her – having her on. I didn't really pay much attention to what she was saying or doing until she said "Amen." It was then it came to my notice that when I went to move my shoulder it was loose; all the pain had gone. But there was this funny – I can't really describe it – a sense of mental and emotional numbness that was also there. A complete calm came over my body. I've never experienced anything like it before in my life. It wasn't a heightened sense of anything. Instead, I was immersed in an incredible sense of contentment. It was like we're all born with dreams and ideals of how we'd like it to be, or what we want to attain, and it was like I'd accomplished all of them at once. Everything I've ever wanted was there, everything I've ever wanted to accomplish, I'd done. I had no worries, no financial concerns, no problems, nothing bothered me the way it used to. I was totally trouble free I was euphoric. The closest thing I can say it was like was ecstasy – but you probably don't want to put that in your book.

After I left the girl behind, my mother picked me up after work in her car and I could not stop smiling despite all my efforts to do so. My mother actually commented, she was quite surprised by how I looked. "How come you've got this funny looking grin on your face. You look so happy. What's going on?" To which I replied, "I don't know, but I can't stop smiling and I feel all tingly." This feeling lasted for one or two hours. I also found myself to be full of energy, a feeling that was always absent after a long, hard day at work. I also told her I'd just been prayed for and she treated it the way I would've a few hours earlier – a bit skeptically.

Looking back on the event, what really struck me was that I hadn't "attained" it in any way. I hadn't studied for it, hadn't worked for it, I just "got it." At the time, I didn't examine the whole situation. All I could comprehend was that one minute some girl was talking to God and putting her hands on my shoulder, and the next this amazing feeling was upon me.

From this I got curious about God and what I'd experienced, for when I thanked the girl for what she'd done she made it clear it was from God, not her. I'd just finished reading *The Celestine Prophecy* and so I suppose I had an awareness that there were some forces out there. I was also being challenged on a daily basis by the Christian girl at work and I was starting to ask myself some of the more important questions in life.

Since then I explored going to church. Some of the ones I went to were totally dead. I'm in a good one now, although there are some people who I wonder whether or not they've ever experienced God the way I did, as they don't seem very alive to me. I am now marrying the Christian girl and acknowledge this event as being a major turning point in my life.

– Bank clerk aged 25 (23 at the time of the experience)

Because it is a work of fiction, it is highly unlikely that a book such as *The Celestine Prophecy*[1] would be given serious consideration in theological or academic circles. Throughout the manuscript the author explores the concept of being guided by an unseen hand. Readers are escorted through a set of seemingly random occurrences, an unfolding series of "coincidences" which later turn out to be fate-inspired insights. Many people readily identify with this universal "guidance" theme, recognizing the times they too have felt guided by unknown forces. This high recognition factor explains some of the enormous success the book and its sequels have had. Although it's not particularly well written, the story is so engaging it has struck a chord with tens of thousands. It especially appeals to younger readers who are searching for clues to their destiny. When my oldest son read it in his early 20s he found it extraordinarily inspiring. It is one of many such books, both fiction and nonfiction, that tap into the tremendous desire for nondogmatic, nonproselytizing, inclusive explorations of spirituality and spiritual experiences.

Booksellers know their market and make their money catering to the appetites of those hungry for such soul food. Medieval and Celtic spirituality are popular and becoming more so. There is a resurgence of interest in such Christian mystics as Julian of Norwich, Meister Eckhart, Teresa of Avila, Catherine of Siena, St. Francis of Assisi, Theresa of Lisieux, Hildegard of Bingen, and such writings as the *Cloud of Unknowing*. A few publishing experts have predicted that this kind of religious publishing will grow exponentially in the next few years. Especially popular will be books related to women mystics, of whom there is no shortage. The mystic's experience of God and the way they describe their divine love affairs strikes a very familiar chord with many a contemporary soul. Often it is these mystical transcendent texts that best match the exquisite soul affairs so many of us have experienced.

Along with the printed word there is another mainstream medium that allows unfettered exploration into the worlds of mystery, spirituality, and soul affairs – movies. Reaching an even broader audience than books and dressed up as popular entertainment, the spiritual legitimacy of movies would certainly be challenged by the religiously orthodox. The public, too, might find it odd to consider movies as any sort of spiritual forum. Nevertheless, here at the heart of our popular culture we find a continual exploration of the great spiritual questions that surround the human condition.

George Miller, the producer of such films as *Babe, Lorenzo's Oil* and *Mad Max,* and the director of *Contact* and *The Witches of Eastwick* goes so far as to call cinemas the temples of our times.

It fascinates me that one of the world's best-kept secrets is how cinemas have become our new covert cathedrals. I believe cinema is now the most powerful secular religion, and people gather in cinemas to experience things collectively, the way they once did in church.

The cinema storytellers have become the new priests. They're doing a lot of the work of our religious institutions, which have so concretised the metaphors in their stories, taken so much of the poetry, mystery and mysticism out of religious belief, that people look for other places to question their spirituality. I don't think we fully understand yet the need of people to gather together to listen to a story, and the power of that act.[2]

A quick glance at any major movie list will illustrate George Miller's point. *The Devil's Advocate* highlights the insidious and seductive nature of evil. *Pretty Woman, The Scent of a Woman, Good Will Hunting, Shakespeare in Love, Eyes Wide Shut, Life Is Beautiful* and dozens of other quality movies explore the theme of true love and compassion. *Dead Man Walking, Mississippi Burning*, and *The Shawshank Redemption* are just a few that explore justice. *Jurassic Park, Titanic* and many other such "disaster" movies illustrate the Judeo-Christian message that our attempts to rely on human technology (storing up treasure, having faith in our own efforts) are doomed; there are forces which humans can never conquer or control and it is folly to believe otherwise. *The Priest, Jesus of Montreal, The Mission* and *The Last Temptation of Christ* frankly question areas of Christianity that are seldom if ever broached by the church. For those willing to search there are deep spiritual truths in many such stories. The list is endless.

When it comes to depicting soul affairs, George Miller's own film about extraterrestrial intelligence does a particularly good job. In *Contact* we see unfolding on the screen a perfect portrayal of the incredible difficulty of explaining something ineffable and indescribable. Towards the end of the film, Jodie Foster's character, Ellie Arroway, a hardheaded, empirically based astronomer, is transported via a space ship/time machine to another dimension of reality. There she ends up on a dreamy tropical beach where her long-dead father appears to her. She asks him questions about how he got there, who put him there, and what is going on, but he doesn't know the answers. All he knows is that his "form" is one "they" chose to show Ellie, so that she wouldn't be completely overwhelmed and terrified.

When Ellie returns to earth, she tries to relate what she observed in an objective, fact based, scientific way. She is not believed. We the audience have seen and been with her on her "trip" and we, like Ellie, experience the journey as being of 18 hours duration. However, those remaining on earth saw her craft fall for a few seconds from its platform into the sea several hundred meters below. They simply can't believe her story of visiting this strange land for so long. It does not match their perception of what really happened. She cannot explain the time differences and being a good scientist cannot be drawn into making conclusions or interpreting her experience. All she can do is relate what happened. The interesting thing is that even the characters playing the religious experts don't believe her, as the language she uses and the events she describes do not fit their criteria of an experience of God. Ellie experienced something outside the prevailing language and conceptual framework of her culture. No one can relate to it, understand it, or even measure it. Uncorroborated, her testimony is dismissed. Despite all her worldly scientific credentials, she is treated as slightly unhinged by it all and is advised not to push her version of events too far, lest she be judged mentally unstable. Sound familiar?

The fictional events depicted in *Contact* highlight a profound truth, not about what Ellie experienced on her trip, but about how a unique inexplicable experience is regarded by the uninitiated. Had we, the audience, not witnessed Ellie's journey, we too would not have believed her story. Seeing is believing. Ellie, like so many prophets and mystics throughout time, and like those who experience soul affairs today, encountered firsthand what happens to those who step outside the current norms. In those moments, she would have known what it felt like to be Noah trying to tell people there was going to be a flood, when they'd never even seen rain; or like the women who claimed they'd seen Christ alive and well, even though he'd been publicly executed a few days before. When it's "impossible," people simply don't believe.

But what our senses perceive to be accurate information may in fact be nowhere near the truth. A short Buddhist story illustrates this problem.

A young widower, who loved his five-year-old son very much, was away on business when bandits came, burned down his whole village, and took his son away. When the man returned to the ruins, he panicked. He took the charred corpse of an infant to be his own child, and he began to pull his hair and beat his chest, crying uncontrollably. He organised a cremation ceremony, collected the ashes and put them in a very beautiful velvet bag. Working, sleeping, eating, he always carried the bag of ashes with him.

One day his real son escaped from the robbers and found his way home. He arrived at his father's new cottage at midnight, and knocked at the door. You can imagine at that time, the young father was still carrying the bag of ashes and crying. He asked, "Who is there?" And the child answered, "It's me, Papa. Open the door, it's your son." In his agitated state of mind the father thought that some mischievous boy was making fun of him, and he shouted at the child to go away, and he continued to cry. The boy knocked again and again, but the father refused to let him in. Some time passed, and finally the child left. From that time on, father and son never saw one another.

After telling this story, the Buddha said, "Sometime, somewhere you take something to be the truth. If you cling to it so much, when the truth comes in person and knocks at your door, you will not open it.[3]

Most people who have had a passionate affair of the soul and who have then tried to explain it would readily identify with this story. Many of the correspondents in this book have described how their soul affairs were received with skepticism or ridicule, or were simply not believed. Part of the problem is our frustrating inability to explain our affairs in ways others might in any way relate to.

I wanted to tell them so much what had happened, to try to get them to grasp the emotion I felt at the time. It was so good I wanted everyone to have it! I believed that everyone has the potential to experience what had happened to me and I wanted it for them too. It would have been selfish to keep it to myself. I felt bottled up because no matter how I tried I just couldn't get it across.

– Male technician aged 32

Spanish mystic St. John of the Cross described it this way.

We receive this mystical knowledge of God clothed in none of the kinds of images, in none of the sensible representations which our mind makes use of in other circumstances. Accordingly in this knowledge, since the senses and the imagination are not employed, we get neither form nor impression, nor can we give any account or furnish any likeness, although the mysterious and sweet-tasting wisdom comes home so clearly to the inmost parts of our soul. Fancy a man seeing a certain kind of thing for the first time in his life. He can understand it, use and enjoy it, but he cannot apply a name to it, nor communicate any idea of it, even though all the while it be a mere thing of sense. How much greater will be his powerlessness when it goes beyond the senses! This is the peculiarity of the divine language. The more infused, intimate, spiritual, and supersensible it is, the more does it exceed the senses, both inner and outer, and impose silence upon them. The soul then feels as if placed in a vast and profound solitude, to which no created thing has access, in an immense and boundless desert, the more delicious the more solitary it is.[4]

Due to their profound ineffability, perhaps the best means of communicating the impact of our soul affairs is not through explanation but through the medium of stories. George Miller's notion that myths, fables, and stories provide the best means for learning great religious and spiritual truths is not new; George Bernard Shaw, writing in the early part of the 20th century, commented that "All the sweetness of religion is conveyed to the world by the hands of storytellers and image-makers. Without their fictions the truths of religion would for the multitude be neither intelligible nor even apprehensible; and the prophets would prophesy and the teachers teach in vain."[5]

As Christ, Buddha, and countless mystics have shown, storytelling is an ideal vehicle for communicating spiritual truths. Perhaps this is one of the reasons why all cultures have long traditions of storytelling. The Irish say that a good story fills the belly. Inuit say that stories chop off half the winter. Stories can embrace and depict our soul affairs in ways argument and exposition never can. We are no different from the campfire storytellers of old, we just use more sophisticated mediums. It is the right-brained artistic mediums – theater, film, literature, art, drama, poetry, and music – where patterns of meaning and interconnectedness become clearer. Here is where ineffable experiences such as soul affairs stand the best chance of being accepted and understood.

Take for example the story told in *The Green Mile*, a movie set in a prison on death row. This film depicts miraculous healings and even a resurrection from the dead! Because it is a story and not a logical exposition, there is no explanation of the events depicted, neither does the audience have to make belief statements about them. We simply become involved in a story. A film such this not only gives us an insight into miraculous soul affairs, but also enriches our lives by giving us food for thought on justice, compassion, good, and evil.

When soul affairs are told in the language of storytelling, we willingly suspend our disbelief and accept information that would be unpalatable in another form. Millions of movie goers who saw the film *The Matrix* would probably have been unaware that they were actually watching a "messiah" story. The movie explores the idea that you won't know your true potential until you take the totally radical step of giving up everything you own, everything you are, even life itself. It is in taking such a revolutionary course that you will not only be released to save your own life, but also the lives of many others – the Christ story in a nutshell. Expressed in religious language, the secular world would reject it. When told as a story, it became a box office hit.

I've highlighted films as a storytelling vehicle because film-making is my craft and because films are familiar to me, but I know there are just as many examples of soul affairs and spiritually inspiring stories in literature, both in fiction and in biography: *A Christmas Carol, The Power of One, Angela's Ashes*, and *City of Joy* represent only a tiny few.

Whatever the medium, the common denominator is the story. The documentary films I have made tell real life stories of courage, and simple truths. My colleagues in the feature film industry tell similar stories with fictional characters and added dramatic effects to entertain, move, and inspire.

When we read stories or watch movies, we care little about how they are made: the subplots, what genre they are in, the editing, publishing details, or which historical author or filmmaker was a key influence on the director or author. These things interest the critic and the academic. What we want is to be engrossed in an engaging narrative. How the filmmaker or storyteller achieves this is irrelevant. Imagine how long people would continue to go to the cinema if, instead of seeing a feature movie, they were shown a video presentation or given a lecture by a film critic or academic pointing out why the film is important! Perhaps that seems farfetched. However, in many churches and academic settings, investigations or excursions into spirituality are presented via lengthy expositions of scriptural texts and theology, rather than via stories which help us make sense of our spiritual experiences. I concur with George Miller when he says that in abdicating its role as storyteller the church has missed the boat. Theologians, religious scholars, and to a large extent the clergy, are to religion and soul affairs what critics and academics are to movies, theater, and literature. There is a place for these people but it isn't on the front lines. That is the domain of the storyteller.

Along with stories, another frequently accessed medium that embraces our soul affairs is music. Music and songs give expression to the deepest yearnings of our souls, bypassing our logical selves to move us in ways our intellectual faculties seldom do. Songs lodge in an especially reserved place within ourselves. Somewhere, somehow, the music penetrates and sticks in our consciousness at a level of knowing totally different from intellectual understanding. Alzheimer's sufferers who cannot string two words together can, when played a tune, sing a whole song word perfect. Songs are a spiritual sacrament in which we all unconsciously and instinctively partake. If we want to make sense of the ultimate reality of our soul affairs, we need only look to the stories and wonderful songs our society produces in volumes. They are second to none in their ability to plug us into another dimension, one that is most likely closer to the euphoric and mysterious times of our soul affairs than our everyday, logical way of processing information.

Songs can sometimes play a part in people's soul affairs. Almost out of nowhere, a few lyrics suddenly bubble up and give expression to what has transpired.

I'd been feeling down and overwhelmed for a few days. I felt too much was being asked of me by too many people. Feeling emotionally fragile, I'd done very little all day. To salve my conscience and to help me forget my troubles, I decided to do some housework. Just before the kids came home from school I was vacuuming furiously and out of nowhere came the image of me running off into the sunset with God. The sense of abandonment was wonderful. There was no sense of it being a suggestion, needing a response from me like, "Will you do this? Yes or no?" The image was just there. It was not a reaction to the drudgery of housework or responsibilities of family or anything like that.

That night I woke up at 4 a.m. I didn't get back to sleep. A song kept going around in my head. It was about not being afraid, that God's love was much stronger than my fear. It was the first song we had sung at a Eucharist the previous Sunday night. I didn't really need to hear it, as I didn't feel afraid anymore. But it was reassuring anyway – like the last link in the chain.

This image I had, I don't think it was something I'm being asked to do. I guess it was just that for those fleeting moments, in a way that is hard to describe but I know in myself to be true, everything was in its proper place. Perhaps it was a sense of being home. God and I were one. Nothing else mattered.

–Woman aged 42

Music has always played a spiritual role. From simple chants to full choral hymns, it has figured prominently in religious activities. Throughout my life, songs have acted as a guiding spiritual inner voice, penetrating my thick hide and getting under my skin in ways few logical arguments could. When I seek solitude, it is these, almost half a century of song lines stored in my head, that well up inside me and somehow give expression to the well-being, inexpressible awe, and interconnectedness I feel with the "All."

Van Morrison, in particular, has given voice to my spiritual longings and desires. His music has accompanied my own life through its varied ups and downs. At every twist and turn there was a "Van the Man" song that seemed to fit. Professional highs and lows, love, longing, and otherness – each new album had at least one track that echoed where I was at emotionally, psychologically, and spiritually. Steeped in Irish tradition, Van's songs of exile, of home, his songs about a deity I could relate to showed me that I was not alone in how I saw things. His music went directly to my heart speaking eloquently in a language I instinctively understood. Although I've never met the man, I consider him a soulmate.

In one of his rare interviews, Van described himself as a Christian mystic. The label certainly fits. Songs such as *Into the Mystic, A Sense of Wonder,* and *Hymns to the Silence,* are on a par with the writings of the ancient mystics. They give voice to what it is like to be loved *by* and in love *with* nature, God, and the "All." Van often sings about healing (*Did Ye Get Healed? The Healing Game, Till We Get the Healing Done*) – the emotional and spiritual healing we all yearn for, the healing and restoration of our souls. Like those of the ancient mystics, his meanings are often obscure and interchangeable. Whether his lover is human or divine doesn't matter, we take from it what we want. For me, Van beautifully expresses the deep yearning for the divine that aches in the hearts and minds of so many human beings, what French philosopher Jean-Paul Sartre described as a "God-shaped hole."

An especially poignant Van Morrison song for me was "Joey Boy," from his album *Avalon Sunset*. Set to a simple, traditional Irish tune, he sings of going back to sit beside the mountain streams of his youth, there to remember a time before yearning was known, when contentment and peace were the norm. Being a migrant myself, my heart strings were plucked as I heard him sing of going back to uncomplicated forms of work and play, a return to the place that fed dreams, dreams which had become tarnished over time through cynicism, sophistication, and hard work. I took it as a personal call to review my life. *Joey Boy* was my invitation to go "home." It became a theme song for me, playing over and over in my mind, orienting me to start a journey that would eventually lead me back to the mountains of my youth, there to sit in silence and solitude for over five weeks, experiencing the soul affairs that were to change my life.

CHAPTER FOURTEEN

COMING HOME

The only certain proof a young woman's friends have that she has lost her virginity is that she is pregnant. Otherwise, there is no proof – not even if she should talk and behave lewdly. Her husband may be impotent.

In the same way, if a soul speaks of God with words of faith and love, either publicly or inwardly, this is no proof either for others or for itself. It may be that what it calls God is an impotent being – that is to say, a false God, and that it has never really slept with God. What is proof is the appearance of supernatural virtues in that part of its behaviour which is turned towards men.

The faith of a judge is not seen in his behaviour at church, but in his behaviour on the bench.

– Simone Weil[1]

Most spiritual traditions hold that transforming moments, religious experiences, theophanies, holy instants, soul affairs, whatever they are labeled, are only genuine if the person's life demonstrates virtues that were previously lacking. However, like all human behavior, the display of a positive change is a continuum, a bell-shaped curve, with obvious dramatic "saintly" change at one end of the spectrum, little noticeable outward change at the other, and the bulk of the population falling somewhere in between. This was evidenced in the British survey, where almost three-quarters of the respondents said that the longer-term outcome of their experience was that it changed their attitude on life to some extent.

However, attitudinal change is sometimes hard to measure. With soul affairs, it is even more difficult due to the deep natural humility that accompanies most experiences. This ensures that even if we do operate in a more virtuous manner, it is highly unlikely we would point it out. Besides, to self-claim virtuous behavior immediately discredits its legitimacy. Even if changes are evident, we will tend to be coy about the reasons, knowing that soul affairs carry little credence and, when expressed in the wrong forum, run the risk of being ridiculed or dismissed. Also, the changes initiated by our affairs, especially those credited to an unseen guiding hand, are likely to be slowly evolving rather than instant and dramatic, the effects seen only in hindsight. Like the small spurt of a spaceship's retro rockets, a slightly altered trajectory at one point puts us into an entirely different orbit. For these reasons the good we do, just like our soul affairs, is generally kept secret.

Many people I spoke to admitted that in having their soul affair something definitely changed. Often they couldn't define it, couldn't say, "Well, before I was like this and now I am like this," or point to their joining the Peace Corps or becoming a street worker. Rather, it was as if they'd had a new operating system installed. Outwardly, they showed little difference, but inwardly the change was profound.

Arthritis has been a major issue in my life for nearly 20 years. Insidiously and relentlessly it strangled life from me. I could no longer play the guitar, no longer play sport. At one stage, I had difficulty dressing myself. I wore joggers summer and winter, to the beach, to work, as my knees and ankles ached even more if I wore any other footwear, and worse if I wore no shoes at all. I wore splints on my wrists to bed every night. One time at a barbecue, my father, with the very best of intentions, cut my steak into bite-sized portions for me, as he knew I would have difficulty doing it myself. He was acting out of love for me, but I felt totally humiliated. After that I always said I preferred sausages.

Because I was generally in poor health, I had difficulty conceiving. When I did have children, I could only breast-feed for a short time, as I had to recommence my drugs. I couldn't get out of a lounge chair with a sleeping baby in my arms, as I needed both hands to push myself up. Some days, the five stairs to the baby's bedroom seemed insurmountable. Later, there were times I cried with frustration as I struggled to get tiny shoes and socks on the feet of a happy, wriggly toddler. Pain was part of every day. Arthritis redefined who I was.

Over the years, I received wonderful help and support from the vast majority of doctors and therapists. One occupational therapist in particular gave me the confidence and practical help I needed to live my life. One doctor commented I was stoic. I was proud of that. At least I was good at enduring pain (if little else). But enduring wasn't enough. I wanted it all to go away. I wanted to be healed. Arthritis wasn't part of the script I had for my life.

My mother-in-law and other well-intentioned relatives and friends of my mother constantly harangued me with the latest miracle cures, as cited by the most recent women's magazine or "current affairs" program on television. I consulted two naturopaths, at different times, for several months and followed their diets and advice. It didn't make any difference.

Then I attended a retreat at a local Christian monastery where a stranger prayed for my healing; he prayed that I would be released from pain and doubt. It was a euphoric moment. I wept. The others around me wept. The atmosphere was so "charged" I fully expected to see my bent fingers straighten before my eyes. But they didn't.

Still, I wasn't disappointed. The euphoria lasted for about three days. I was totally distracted. I couldn't eat. I was shivering for a lot of the time and I felt nauseous. I was on such a high it crossed my mind I might be pregnant. This experience at the monastery was a defining moment for me, in the sense of dividing my life into "before" and "after," as significant as the changes brought about by marriage and having children. From this moment forward, my attitudes, outlook, and sense of priorities were irrevocably changed. I even made several phone calls to people asking for their forgiveness for things I'd done in the past. Somehow I had to get everything straight.

But the arthritis remained.

Over the next few years, I went to healing services and even a three-day healing conference a thousand kilometers away from my home and family. I was sure I would receive some miracle cure during that time. But I didn't. People gave me books to read. For years, friends regularly prayed for me to be healed. My quest for healing became a frustrating exercise. I felt I was a failure. I assumed it was because of some fault in me that all these prayers didn't "work."

It seems now that all this happened a long time ago. But recently I realized that I had in fact been healed. And I'm not even sure when it occurred. Now this claim may appear very strange, because outwardly nothing has changed. I still take drugs, my fingers are still crooked, I still experience pain occasionally and will probably face further surgery. But a few months ago, suddenly, out of the blue, I became aware that I am no longer bound by arthritis. I've been released. It no longer defines me. That's the difference. I didn't abandon my quest for healing – it's just that at some point in the last few years it ceased to be important. And that, I believe, is when I was released. That's when the healing happened. The emotional, physical, and spiritual pain of arthritis no longer overwhelms me.

Most people equate healing with a cure. The paraplegic wakes up one day and is able to run to the corner shop. The person with a brain tumor has a follow-up X-ray and there's no sign of any problem. Or a medical cure. Cataracts are removed, restoring sight. Blocked arteries to the heart are replaced, giving life. This is all miracle territory.

Being healed and being cured are very different. But a healing of the spirit and emotions, as I've received, is no less miraculous. I imagine the victims of physical and sexual abuse can never erase their intensely painful memories. They can never deny the reality of the horror of their abuse. But with time, they can be healed. To be freed from incredible rage, bitterness, feelings of powerlessness – to be able to forgive the terrible wrongs done to them – is a miracle. My pain bears no resemblance to the intensity of theirs, yet I too have been released from what once bound me.

Looking back on it after all this time, it's obvious to me that arthritis wasn't the real issue anyway. That was just my body's response to deeper issues. The stranger's prayer, that I be released from pain and doubt, has been granted. But I realize that healing is an ongoing process. There are other issues in my life from which I need to be healed. A lifetime of other things. Other failures. Other shame. Dark secrets. Wrongs I have done, wrongs that have been done to me. Moments when I have compromised myself to gain acceptance, or cared too much what others think. Hurts I haven't dealt with. Unresolved conflict. Jealousy, arrogance, lust, pettiness, pride. Worry. Times I haven't been able to forgive myself for my weakness or ineptitude. False self-accusation. Being too attached to people or to things. I need to deal with all these and let them go. In clinging to them, I prevent myself from being healthy and whole.

I read somewhere that we all have two sources of divine power in our lives. One is the capacity to forgive and the other is the ability to endure suffering with patience. I look at my crooked fingers and am thankful now for the course my life has taken. It is not how I envisaged it would be. But as I continue my journey towards wholeness I am very grateful for this path I was thrust upon.

– Woman aged 37 at the time of her experience

The overriding impression I got from those who'd had a soul affair was that above all else it was the way they viewed life that had changed. As the above example shows, how that altered state might manifest itself is as individual as each one of us. However, one thing I did detect in many soul affair veterans was an absence of longing. When speaking about their soul affairs, many did so with a quiet certainty. There was a lack of drivenness, a simple peacefulness. Although they were more than willing to talk, many were disinterested in explaining or justifying their experiences. It did not seem to matter what others thought. It was their own affair, their private moment, their secret. The experience itself was enough.

One accusation which is often leveled against those who have had transcendent soul affairs is that the recipient dwells on the soul affair as an end in itself, seeking the experience again and again for its intrinsic pleasure. Although undoubtedly there are some individuals who do this, I found no basis for believing this to be a general pattern. I met no one who actively re-sought the experience for the thrill they might get. Although many admitted it would be wonderful if it happened again, they seemed to instinctively understand it was not their call. Most treated their secret affair as a special gift.

Some said their religious convictions had been confirmed and strengthened. Some said it affirmed their faith, making it deeper but less well defined. Others completely rejected a religious explanation. Regardless of the individual interpretations, the overwhelming majority felt they were better people because of their affair. Feeling good about oneself may sound selfish and inward looking, but in gaining inner peace and contentment they found they were freer to think less about themselves and to look more towards others.

Since my time in the mountains, my life has taken subtle but important turns. I am taking new journeys that fill my soul with a deep sense of satisfaction, the like of which I had only occasionally encountered before. Maybe it is just because I'm mellowing with age; maybe it's because my children have grown up and left home and my responsibility for them has lessened; maybe it's because I have a credible record of achievement in my chosen field. But I had all these things before I entered the mountains, yet I still felt something was lacking. Indeed, it was because I felt empty and hollow that I was propelled into my first journey of solitude.

Since that time, I have returned to the same mountainous region on my own for several long periods. Each time I go an entirely new spiritual adventure unfolds as I get drawn deeper and more intimately into the amazing mystery of the All. Interspersed with these long weeks of solitude are shorter times of a few days, usually at a friend's beach house about an hour's drive from where I live. I cannot tell you what I achieve in these times. Neither can I state why I do it. I simply relish these soul feeding times, restoring as they do my depleted soul capital.

What is different for me since my mountain soul affair is that I am now far more willing to go forward without knowing the outcome. Whereas before I constantly evaluated the destination before moving on, these days I am more committed to the process and to simply enjoying the journey.

Like the young man in the Sufi story of the pearl and the dragon, I too returned as an older man to see if the mountain experiences of my youth were valid. There I rediscovered the "pearl" of great price and saw that the "dragon" that guarded the pearl was of my own making – my ambitions, pride, judgmental attitudes and my fears of other people's opinions of me. Every now and then in day-to-day life, the dragon comes back to attack me as the fear of letting others down or missing a deadline wells up inside. But the fear passes. These days I don't see myself as being so individually responsible for my fate. I think it's called faith. Faith, not that bad things will not happen, for they do, but faith that I now accept I am a tiny part of a much bigger, unfathomable whole.

Being more ruled by my heart than my head has led to subtle but important changes in all aspects of my life, especially my work. As I write these lines, I am overlooking the Nuku'alofa fore-shore on the tiny Pacific island of Tonga. I'm here for two weeks as part of an Australian Aid project, the Pacific Media Initiative, to train and help prepare Tongan radio staff for their launch into television in a few weeks' time. It is my third stint doing aid work in the Pacific in the last 12 months. Six months ago, I was at a community TV station in Fiji training staff who, with the most primitive equipment and minimal funds, manage to run a TV network that beams programs in Hindi, Fijian, and English to an audience of 80,000. A few months prior to that, Christine and I spent six weeks in Samoa training a local production team to make a television cooking series aimed at raising the nutritional levels of children's diets. Whether I would be involved in this aid work if I hadn't had a soul affair is debatable since Christine and I have a long history of being involved in Third World issues. But although I would have been willing, I doubt I would have been available.

There's a saying in the TV industry that you're only as good as your last film. In other words, if you make a dud, it is highly likely you'll be sidelined. Consequently, I tended to energetically pursue opportunities to make TV programs and documentaries. I kept busy on the freelance circuit lobbying for a chance to make films – films that would both engage me and the audience and also act as stepping stones to other programs, ones that would reach a bigger audience and impact on many more lives. I was extremely busy and my diary was always full.

Since my mountain soul affair, I have not worked on a TV program or made a documentary film. Instead, my work has been writing books and articles, and producing TV commercials and videos for corporate clients – gigs that certainly don't look wonderful on a documentary filmmaker's curriculum vitae! That's what has changed for me; it no longer matters so much. There are now gaps in my forward planning diary – big gaps – mostly gaps in fact! This means I am more available to do the work that seems to fulfil my deepest desires.

Our stint in Samoa also set Christine and me on a very different life course. The project was initiated and sponsored by the local Baha'i community. Samoa has one of the seven Baha'i houses of worship in the world and we were the first non-Baha'is allowed to stay within the temple grounds. Set high up on an extinct volcano overlooking the capital, Apia, we were cocooned by the gentle Polynesian rhythms that dictated the running of the temple and its surroundings. I especially loved sitting in the bamboo grove of an evening watching the sun set over the Pacific Ocean. Christine relished the fact that within three weeks of being in Samoa, a simple task such as visiting the bank turned into a three-hour exercise, as it took so long to talk to all the people she now knew! Samoa dislodged us from our cosmopolitan city way of life and made us ripe for a major sea change.

On our way home to Sydney, we detoured via New Zealand for a few days to see the sights, visit a few friends and relatives and see our eldest son who was working on the feature film *The Lord of the Rings*. On the morning we were preparing to fly back home, a strange thing happened.

It was a drop dead gorgeous day, snow on the nearby mountains and not a cloud in the sky. It was too good to rush, so we spent most of the day just cruising around visiting vantage points that provided wonderful panoramic views. On our travels, we came across a farm that was carved into blocks for sale. We used real estate "hunting" as an excuse to walk to the top of a hill to get a better view. When we got there we were spellbound. This hilltop had the most perfect panoramic view stretching 60-odd kilometers in each direction. But what made it really special was that "my" mountain, the one where I had spent most of my time in solitude, was right in the center!

It was love at first sight. I was reminded as we strolled through the lush green grass that the kingdom of heaven is like a man who discovers a treasure buried in a field, who returns home, sells all he has, and returns to buy the field. There was little head stuff involved. It was a total heart response. We didn't even look over the property to see if it was fenced, had water, or could grow anything. We just bought it. It was a soul moment for both of us.

So we are in the process of selling our suburban Sydney house, winding up our production company, and setting out to claim our treasure buried in this field. How it pans out, what our role will be, how we will earn a living, are all unknowns – but strangely we feel little fear. There is just such a sense of rightness. We do not imagine a comfortable ride. Indeed, life will be full of challenges, frustrations, and be much harder than what we're used to. But we are ready to do whatever it is that we are meant to and we are looking forward to it.

This relocation brings with it some added benefits. We will be on hand to help and support the wife and two young children of a very dear friend who was tragically killed a couple of years ago. We will also be within an hour's drive of my elderly parents. My father suffered a couple of minor heart attacks recently and I'm more aware than ever how limited and precious the time with them is. The small Catholic rural community that attracted me all those years ago is still going strong and is only a short drive away. Perhaps it's time for us to become more involved there. These aren't "reasons" for our move, rather they are things that have cemented our heart decision. We were seduced by the landscape and now other aspects are emerging that affirm the rightness of our choice.

On the spiritual level too, I have crossed over a brand new threshold and have been pushed down a totally different path. It was another soul affair, 18 months after my first mountain episode that culminated in my making a commitment to live life more simply and to spread the spirit of love and harmony. This is the essence of the vows I have taken as a tertiary Franciscan. Founded by St. Francis in the 13th century, this secular or third order is for those who are called to the religious life but who cannot take literal vows of poverty, chastity, and obedience. (No money, no honey, and no funny business, as one brother jokingly told me!) In the same way that many Westerners are more comfortable with the mystery-friendly Eastern and Celtic traditions, I have found fellow travellers amongst these followers of St. Francis and St. Clare. Drawing on more than eight centuries of tradition, my spiritual colleagues encourage and support the less well-defined, more spiritually inclined journeys so many of us are on. It is amongst such reflective, contemplative souls I now feel most at home.

The soul affair that precipitated my journeying down the Franciscan path was a loving call back to my religious home, the one I was born into, the one I fled from all those years ago. Like an immigrant who returns to their native country after many decades away, I have discovered that the rituals and traditions I so disliked as a youth are an integral part of me. With hindsight I can see that running away from church as a youngster into the mountains was a running towards something that took decades to unfold. It was there in the solitude and silence of nature that I was met by that indefinable mystery some call God, and others call a presence or power. I now realize that the church cave I ran away from actually *does* harbor in its deepest recesses, covered by cobwebs, mud, and obscure religious rhetoric, a pearl of great price. As long as I am vigilant in giving authority to the pearl, and not to the dragons of fear and fundamentalism, I stand a good chance of not being attacked.

In the process of reflecting on my own and others' soul affairs, I have had to re-examine the religious roots of my own culture. In better understanding conventional Western religion, I have become more accepting of it, although these days I participate in unconventional ways. I have always enjoyed going to churches and temples when no one else is there. The decades, sometimes centuries of prayer and reverence that have transpired in those spaces by thousands of pilgrims, impart a fragrance of peace, an essence of holiness that is almost palpable. When I spend time there in quiet reflection, I gain inspiration, courage, and a sense of being part of something unfathomably bigger than human endeavor. I love hearing religious songs and prayers in languages I do not understand. Taizé singing especially satisfies. When I don't understand, I stop searching for meaning, stop arguing and debating, and instead listen with my heart, feeling the emotions being expressed: veneration, joy, holiness, stillness, and peace. Not understanding brings out my child heart in me. It is as a vulnerable child that I feel closest to The Source, the delicious mystery.

Most weeks, an ex-Catholic priest friend and I attend a small, intimate, midday mass deep in the crypt of a nearby monastery. Neither of us is "legally" entitled to take the sacraments, but that does not bother us or the celebrants. As many of the novices are

Pacific Islanders, the a cappella singing is simple, rich, and beautiful. Unlike parish life, there are no administrative matters to be dealt with, no collections to be taken, and conversation, although not forbidden, is rarely engaged in. We are all there for the main game – the sharing of a 2,000-year-old ritual. What this intensely personal and private affair means to each one of us is entirely different. Afterwards, my friend and I go back to his apartment and share a simple midday meal consisting of a loaf of freshly baked bread. Such simplicity is in itself enough. I always go away enriched. My soul restored again.

***

After more than three years of wading through the myriad of deeply disguised religious labyrinths that surround soul affairs, I have come to realize there is no authority on the subject. We are all on an equal footing. As Carl Jung commented, "Every statement about the transcendent ought to be avoided because it is a laughable presumption on the part of the human mind, unconscious of its limitations."[2] The conclusions we make about affairs of the soul are not all that relevant as it is a highly subjective area and no conclusion could ever suffice. What is important, though, is an awareness of all the factors that prevent us from disclosing, let alone openly discussing this most profound and universal human experience.

Few reputable studies on the topic have been undertaken. In fact, there is so little academic or religious analysis of Western experiential spirituality that an intellectual vacuum surrounds the subject. Most researchers in the field, both in academia and in religion, are mainly interested in studying the spiritual experiences of professed religious. Missing from the literature are the profound religious, spiritual, and transcendent experiences of ordinary people – many of whom never attend religious services and who might well describe themselves as anti-religious or irre-

214 — SECRET AFFAIRS OF THE SOUL

ligious. So little study has been done on the topic it is assumed that few people experience a presence or power, whether they call it God or not. Therefore, in a circular argument, it seems unworthy of serious research. Consequently, it is off the agendas of those studying the psychology and sociology of religion. This further serves to reduce experiential spirituality's credibility. With so few serious studies done, soul affairs are easily dismissed or lumped in with superstition, mental illness, and magic despite the fact that the overwhelming majority of experiences definitely do not fit in these categories.

When it comes to initiating, understanding, or predicting soul affairs, we are in a spiritual and religious no man's land, for soul affairs occur spontaneously. There are no formulas or ways to precipitate them, they just happen. They aren't earned and we can't work or study for them. We can hope, wish, and pray for them, but there are no guarantees. There is no way of summoning them. No one can foresee when and to whom they will occur. Like the random quirks of nature, they are totally out of our control.

Due to the ineffability of soul affairs combined with the public disbelief and ignorance that surrounds them, it is likely they will remain secret for some time yet. Nevertheless, they are perhaps the truest, most profound and potentially life changing experiences we will ever have. If you have had an affair of the soul, I trust that in reading about others' affairs you, like me, have gained solace that you are not alone, deluded, or mentally unhinged, and that you recognize that we have simply experienced something which is an integral part of the human condition. If this point alone is reached, my work is done.

***

If you would like to read further accounts of soul affairs or contribute one of your own, visit the author's soul affairs website at **www.soulaffairs.com**

ENDNOTES

Introduction

[1] John Steinbeck, *Of Mice and Men* (London: Heineman Educational Books, New Windmill Series, 1965).

Chapter 1

[1] Dag Hammarskjöld, *Markings* (New York: Random House, 1966). Reproduced in *The Columbia Dictionary of Quotations* (New York: Columbia University Press, 1995).

Chapter 2

[1] Quoted in Philipp Frank, *Einstein: His Life and Times*, ch.12, sct. 5. From *The Columbia Dictionary of Quotations* (New York: Columbia University Press, 1995).

[2] Margaret Smith, *An Introduction to Mysticism* (London: Sheldon Press, 1977) p. 10.

[3] M. D. A. Deikman, "Biomodal Consciousness and the Mystic Experience" in *Understanding Mysticism*, ed. R. Woods (London: Althone Press, 1981) p. 266.

Chapter 3

[1] Henri-Frédéric Amiel, *Journal Intime* (1882: tr. by Mrs. Humphry Ward, 1892), entry for 27 October 1856. From *The Columbia Dictionary of Quotations* (New York: Columbia University Press, 1995).

Chapter 4

[1] Salman Rushdie, in the *Independent*, London, 7 February 1990. From *The Columbia Dictionary of Quotations* (New York: Columbia University Press, 1995).

[2] Alister Hardy, *The Spiritual Nature of Man* (Oxford: Oxford University Press, 1979) p. 1.

[3] Ibid., p. 3.

[4] Ibid., p. 4.

[5] Account number 183, the Alister Hardy Archives, Westminster College, Oxford, UK. All other accounts taken from the Alister Hardy Archives will be followed by the account number in parenthesis.

[6] Hardy, *Spiritual Nature of Man*, p. 113.

[7] David Hay, *Exploring Inner Space: Scientists and Religious Experience* (Oxford: A. R. Mowbray & Co. Ltd., 1987) p. 123.

[8] Ibid., p. 136.

[9] Reported in *The Sydney Morning Herald*, Australia, 14 August 1997.

Chapter 5

[1] Shankara as quoted in Aldous Huxley, *The Perennial Philosophy* (London: Chatto & Windus, 1946) p. 13.

[2] Abraham Maslow, *Religions, Values, and Peak Experiences* (Middlesex: Penguin, 1964) p. 28.

[3] Ibid., p. vii.

[4] M. Scott Peck, *Denial of the Soul* (New York: Simon & Schuster, 1997) p. 124.

[5] Hay, *Inner Space*, p. 163.

[6] Ibid.

[7] Ibid.

Chapter 6

[1] Arthur Koestler, *The Act of Creation* (New York: Arkana, 1990) pt.2, ch. 8. Reproduced in *The Columbia Dictionary of Quotations* (New York: Columbia University Press, 1995).

Chapter 7

[1] From the Internet

[2] Hay, *Inner Space*, pp. 148–9, 165.

[3] Ibid., p156. All further accounts taken from Hay's volume *Inner Space*, will be followed by the page number in parenthesis.

[4] Ibid., p. 150.

[5] Ibid., pp. 150, 157.

[6] Ibid., p. 130.

[7] Ibid., pp. 132, 134.

[8] USA Evangelical Press News Service, 8 September 1998.

[9] Hay, *Inner Space*, p. 130.

[10] Michael Mason, unpublished survey, Melbourne, Australia.

[11] Hay, *Inner Space*, p. 128.

[12] Ibid., p. 134.

[13] Ibid., p. 166.

[14] Ibid., pp. 148–149.

[15] Ibid., p. 124. (USA Gallup poll)

[16] Mason, unpublished survey.

[17] Reginald W. Bibby, *Unknown Gods: The Ongoing Story of Religion in Canada* (Toronto: Stoddart Publishing, 1993) p. 132.

Chapter 8

[1] Victor Hugo, *Les Miserables* (1862) pt. 2, bk. 7, ch. 1. Reproduced in *The Columbia Dictionary of Quotations* (New York: Columbia University Press, 1995).

Chapter 9

[1] Evelyn Underhill, *The Mystics of the Church* (London: James Clarke & Co. Ltd., 1925) p. 215.

[2] Stephen Clissold, *The Wisdom of the Spanish Mystics* (London: Sheldon Press, 1977) pp. 43–44.

[3] Sabina Flanagan, "Hildegard of Bingen, 1098–1179" in *Hildegard of Bingen: A Visionary Life* (London: Routledge, 1989) p. 4.

[4] Underhill, *Mystics*, p. 76.

[5] Richard M. Bucke, *Cosmic Consciousness: A Study in the Evolution of the Human Mind* quoted in William James, *The Varieties of Religious Experience: A Study in Human Nature* (London: Longmans, Green, and Co., 1907) p. 399.

[6] 2 Kings 6:17 (New International Version)

[7] Acts 2:2 (New International Version)

[8] Clissold, *Spanish Mystics*, pp. 29–30.

[9] *The Routledge Encyclopedia of Philosophy*, Vol. 6 (London: Routledge, 1998)

[10] Genesis 16:13 (New International Version)

[11] Jonathan Kirsch, *The Harlot by the Side of the Road: Forbidden Tales of the Bible* (London: Random House, 1997) p. 51.

[12] *The Sunday Times*, reprinted in *The Australian*, November 1997.

[13] Timothy Freke, *The Illustrated Book of Sacred Scriptures* (New Alresford, UK: Godsfield Press, 1998) p. 14.

[14] Peter France, *Hermits: The Insights of Solitude* (London: Random House, 1996) pp. 216–217.

[15] Peggy Noonan, *What I Saw at the Revolution* (1990) ch. 13. Reproduced in *The Columbia Dictionary of Quotations* (New York: Columbia University Press, 1995).

[16] William James, *The Varieties of Religious Experience: A Study in Human Nature* (London: Longmans, Green and Co., 1907) pp. 67–68.

[17] Ibid., pp. 72–73.

[18] Ibid., pp. 66–67.

Chapter 10

[1] Lucinda Vardey, ed. *God in All Worlds: An Anthology of Spiritual Writing* (New York: Millennium Books, 1995) p. xviii.

[2] From the Internet.

[3] Harry R. Moody, David Carroll, *The Five Stages of the Soul* (Sydney: Random House, 1998) p. 160–165.

[4] Hardy, *Spiritual Nature of Man*, p. 65.

[5] John Cornwell, *The Hiding Places of God* (New York: Warner Books, 1991) pp. 192–195.

Chapter 11

[1] Arthur Schopenhauer, as quoted in N. S. Xavier, M.D., *The Two Faces of Religion: A Psychiatrist's View* (Tuscaloosa: Portals Press, 1987).

[2] William D. Hendricks, *Exit Interviews: Revealing Stories of Why People Are Leaving the Church* (Chicago: Moody Press, 1993) pp. 282–283.

[3] Clissold, *The Spanish Mystics*, p. 18.

[4] Ibid., pp. 7–8

[5] Ibid., p. 22.

[6] Paul Harrison, "History of Pantheism," e-mail: harrison@dircon.co.uk.

[7] Bibby, *Unknown Gods*, p. 103.

[8] Peter Bentley and Philip J. Hughes, *Australian Life and the Christian Faith: Facts and Figures* (Christian Research Association, 1998) p. 117.

[9] Bibby, *Unknown Gods*, pp. 6–7.

Chapter 12

[1] Moody and Carroll, *Stages of the Soul*, p. 307.

[2] Bibby, *Unknown Gods*, p. 186.

[3] Ibid., p. 119.

[4] P. Hughes, C. Thompson, R. Pryor, and G. Bouma, *Believe It or Not: Australian Spirituality and the Churches in the '90s* (Melbourne: Christian Research Association, 1995) p. 14.

[5] Hendricks, *Exit Interviews*, p. 249.

[6] Hughes, *Believe It or Not*, p. 11.

[7] M. Scott Peck, *Further Along the Road Less Traveled* (New York: Simon & Schuster, 1993) pp. 243–245.

[8] Bibby, *Unknown Gods*, p. 73.

Chapter 13

[1] James Redfield, *The Celestine Prophecy: An Adventure* (New York: Bantam Doubleday Dell Publishing Group, 1993).

[2] Janet Hawley, "The Hero's Journey," in *The Sydney Morning Herald*, Australia, 14 October 1995, p. 54.

[3] Thich Nhat Hanh, *Being Peace* (Berkeley, Parallax Press, 1987).

[4] St. John of the Cross, *The Dark Night of the Soul* (Paris, 1893), quoted in William James, *Varieties of Religious Experience*, pp. 407–408.

[5] George Bernard Shaw, *Back to Methuselah* (1921) preface. Reproduced in *The Columbia Dictionary of Quotations* (New York: Columbia University Press, 1995).

Chapter 14

[1] George A. Panichas, *The Simone Weil Reader* (New York: David McKay Company, 1977), p. 429.

[2] F. C. Happold, *Mysticism: A Study and an Anthology* (London: Penguin Books, 1963) p. 64.

INDEX

PAUL HAWKER started life in New Zealand where he worked as a cook, truck driver, lineman, mechanic, farm laborer and high school teacher. Since 1979 he has been a professional television writer/director, producing programs and documentaries on topics ranging from social issues and science to shipwrecks and adventure. Most of Paul's films have screened in prime time on Australian television networks. Paul writes and speaks about spirituality, ethics, religion, and the search for meaning. His articles have appeared in Australian and New Zealand magazines and journals. As part of Australia's government-sponsored aid program (AusAID), Paul manages television training workshops in Pacific Island countries. After 15 years of living in Australia Paul and his wife Christine have relocated back to their native New Zealand.

Photo: Christine Hawker

Paul and Christine have three adult sons.